THE PSYCHOLOGY OF MAKING
LIFE INTERESTING

THE MACMILLAN COMPANY
NEW YORK · BOSTON · CHICAGO
DALLAS · ATLANTA · SAN FRANCISCO

MACMILLAN AND CO., LIMITED
LONDON · BOMBAY · CALCUTTA
MADRAS · MELBOURNE

**THE MACMILLAN COMPANY
OF CANADA, LIMITED**
TORONTO

The Psychology of Making Life Interesting

By
WENDELL WHITE, Ph.D.
UNIVERSITY OF MINNESOTA

Author of
THE PSYCHOLOGY OF DEALING WITH PEOPLE
Appealing to the Want for a Feeling
of Personal Worth

NEW YORK
THE MACMILLAN COMPANY

1939

Copyright, 1939, by
THE MACMILLAN COMPANY.

All rights reserved—no part of this book may be reproduced in any form without permission in writing from the publisher, except by a reviewer who wishes to quote brief passages in connection with a review written for inclusion in magazine or newspaper.

Set up and printed. Published April, 1939.
Reprinted August, 1939; October, 1939.

PRINTED IN THE UNITED STATES OF AMERICA
AMERICAN BOOK—STRATFORD PRESS, INC., NEW YORK

PREFACE

THIS is the second book that I have prepared in the field of applied psychology. The first one [1] is devoted to the subject of dealing with people by appealing to the want for a feeling of personal worth. That want, as I showed in the volume devoted to it, exerts a wide and persistent influence over our thoughts and actions. It prompts us to think and to do things; at times to attain a sense of importance; at other times to protect ourselves against a loss of self-regard. The want for a feeling of personal worth is often expressed quite obviously, but usually lies hid in a variety of disguises. It is one of the fundamental human desires, and an understanding of its influence upon the life of man is essential to intelligent human relationships and human management. I discussed that want from the standpoint of dealing with people in life situations in general, from the standpoint of preventing unwholesome behavior (wrongdoing and mental abnormality), and from the standpoint of furthering mental health. I did so because we are interested in problems in all of these classifications, and because there is a definite relationship between them.

This book on the psychology of making life interesting is built around the want for variety, and, like the first book, pertains to the subject of dealing with people

[1] White, Wendell. *The Psychology of Dealing with People.* New York, The Macmillan Company, 1936.

in life situations in general, to preventing unwholesome behavior, and to furthering mental health.

Valuable assistance was received in the writing of this book. Burton Paulu, Robert S. Hilpert and Walter T. Pattison of the University of Minnesota made helpful suggestions for developing certain chapters. Charles L. Bane of the Junior College at Virginia Minnesota and lecturer for the Extension Division of the University of Minnesota, and Claude L. Nemzek of the University of Detroit read most of a late version of the manuscript and suggested many improvements. Haldor B. Gislason of the University of Minnesota was a valuable counselor throughout the writing of this book. Curtis E. Avery of this University carefully studied the entire manuscript in its various stages of development, and in each reading made many valuable criticisms in regard to both subject matter and manner of presentation. I am very grateful to him and to the above mentioned and other colleagues and friends who have assisted me. For contributing toward the development of this book in every way, I am much indebted to my wife, Margaret Byram White.

CONTENTS

	PAGE
PREFACE	v
INTRODUCTION	xiii

PART ONE

DEALING WITH PEOPLE IN LIFE SITUATIONS IN GENERAL

CHAPTER

I. EXPRESSING VARIED THOUGHTS AND ATTITUDES ... 3
    Original expression ... 3
    Unusual remarks made in a light vein ... 5
    Information and news ... 5
    Overstatements made in a light vein ... 6
    Unusualness in fiction ... 6
    Avoidance of uninteresting topics ... 8
    Avoidance of unwanted details ... 8
    Change of subject ... 10
    Silence as a means of giving variety ... 10
    Conversation supplemented with other activity ... 11
    Varied attitudes ... 11
    Individuality ... 14

II. EXPRESSING THOUGHTS IN VARIED WAYS ... 16
    Precision of expression ... 17
    Synonymous terms ... 17
    Novel terms ... 18
    Familiar terms ... 18
    Slang ... 19
    Variation in sentence structure ... 21
    Contrasting ideas ... 25
    Development of a subject in different ways ... 27
    Mental pictures of various senses ... 29
    Expression by means of a silent look ... 34

CONTENTS

CHAPTER		PAGE
III.	AROUSING CURIOSITY	35
	Variety afforded by curiosity	36
	Curiosity-provoking statements	36
	In everyday life	37
	In advertising	37
	In fiction	37
	Sentences having a curiosity-provoking construction	38
IV.	KEEPING UP SUSPENSE	40
	Variety afforded by suspense	40
	Suspense in recreational activity	41
	Suspense in planning something	41
	Suspense in mystery	42
	Suspense in witnessing activity of man or nature	42
	Suspense in fiction and dramatic art	43
V.	GIVING SURPRISE	48
	Variety afforded by surprise	48
	Surprise in paradoxes	49
	Surprise in irony	51
	Surprise in stories and plays	52
	Surprise in comparisons	56
	Surprise in humor	57
VI.	VARYING THE VOICE AND PLAY OF THE FEATURES	60
	Pitch	60
	Quality	61
	Loudness	61
	Rate	62
	Gestures	62
	The influence of emotions upon the voice	63
VII.	VARYING THE DOING OF THINGS OF EVERY KIND	68
	Things of a personal nature	68

CONTENTS

CHAPTER		PAGE
	Things of a public nature	71
	Having different members take part	71
	Providing a varied program	73
	Rearrangement of furniture	73
	Change of program from time to time	74
	Things of a commercial nature	74

Part Two

PREVENTING UNWHOLESOME BEHAVIOR DUE TO TEDIUM

VIII.	Causes of Tedium Underlying Unwholesome Behavior	79
	Monotonous occupations	79
	Idleness	84
	Solitude	86
	Enforced association	87
	Lifelong continuance in motonony	87
IX.	Types of Unwholesome Behavior Due to Tedium	91
	Truancy and vagrancy	91
	The starting of fires for excitement	93
	Combat	94
	Cruelty	95
	Excessive use of alcoholic liquors	95
	Imposition upon another's time	98
	Inquisitiveness	99
	Betting	99
	The making of overstatements in seriousness	100
	Mental abnormalities	100

Part Three

FURTHERING MENTAL HEALTH

X.	Preliminary Statements	105
XI.	Enabling Everyone to Have Something to Do	112

CONTENTS

CHAPTER		PAGE
XII.	AFFORDING OCCASIONAL CHANGE OF WORK	117
	Change of work in industry	117
	Automatic work as a means of giving variety	120
	Change of work in education	123
XIII.	AFFORDING DUE LEISURE FOR ALL	125
	Daily intermissions	128
	Short working days	128
	Week-ends and holidays	129
	Annual vacations	129
XIV.	GETTING THE INDIVIDUAL IN TOUCH WITH NATURE	131
	Variety in nature	131
	The need of developing observation	135
	The need of a window with a view	138
XV.	PROVIDING ACTIVE AND PASSIVE RECREATION	139
	The enjoyment of active recreation	139
	The enjoyment of passive recreation	141
	The lack of opportunity for active recreation	142
	The sponsoring of active recreation by the community	142
XVI.	ENCOURAGING THE PURSUIT OF HOBBIES OR DIVERSIFIED INTERESTS	147
	The benefits of a hobby	147
	Persons who need a hobby	147
	The benefits of diversified activity	152
XVII.	ALLOWING FREEDOM IN LEISURE HOURS	153
XVIII.	MAKING IT POSSIBLE TO MEET PEOPLE	158
	The interest in people	158
	Personal factors determining interest in others	162
	Opportunities for people to mingle	163
	Getting people acquainted	164

CHAPTER		PAGE
XIX.	Affording Opportunity for Change of Scene	167
	The desire for change of scene . . .	167
	The pleasure of change in manner of going about	168
	Change of scene in leisure pursuits . .	169
	Change of scene in pursuing occupations .	169
	The importance to everyone of change of scene	170
XX.	Affording Privacy for Reading and Independent Thought	171
XXI.	Enlarging Experience through Poetry .	178
XXII.	Enlarging Experience through Visual Art	185
XXIII.	Enlarging Experience through Music .	190
XXIV.	Enlarging Experience by Means of Radio Broadcasts	196
XXV.	Conclusion	203
	Self-Testing Exercises	207
	Index	213

INTRODUCTION

LIFE, to be interesting, must have variety. All the senses respond to diversity or change, and in it they frequently find delight. A person who is many-sided or who is different from others gets immediate attention and may be very pleasing; a thing that is diversified or unlike other things is quickly noticed and may be as enjoyable as it is striking. And to anyone, the doing of things that broaden experience gives pleasure. In any type of sensory impression or of activity, variety quickens attention and often makes life interesting.

Another way of looking at man's desire for variety is to view it from the standpoint of his aversion to extreme sameness. The eye grows weary when it has no scope; the ear, when it has no choice; and the mind, when it is engaged in endless routine. Sameness of any kind tends to go unheeded or to make life dull.

The variety that a person has depends upon the complexity and number of his experiences, and upon the degree to which they afford him contrast or novelty.

We desire variety in sensory impressions, in independent thoughts, and in activities. And any one of these general forms of varied experiences, to be enjoyed thoroughly, must frequently involve some change of emotional state. Variety of emotional life, even though it may involve highly exciting instances, is often enjoyed more than is variety of unemotional experiences. To some persons whose lives have been flat, pleasure is where the tempest blows.

Man does not desire variety independently of other values. He likes things that not only give change of experience but that also have intrinsic worth; he likes people who are not simply many-sided or unlike other persons but whose expressions are also in themselves enjoyable to him. And man frequently prefers a familiar experience to a novel one because it brings to mind pleasant remembrances, or because it is less exacting or less hazardous. But everyone desires some change of experience, and no one is interested long in anything wholly unvaried. To a person who has been satiated with sameness, variety of things that are in themselves of little value often gives more pleasure than does uniformity of things of intrinsic worth. As observers in all ages have affirmed, no pleasure endures unseasoned by variety.

Variety not only makes the experiences of life interesting; it also has therapeutic value. Many persons have disturbing thoughts. They may be solicitous of their health, occupation, or relationships with other persons, or they may worry over the condition of someone else in whose well-being they are especially interested. The best treatment for worry is, of course, removal of its cause. But there are cases in which this treatment is impossible. In such a case, the best way to free the individual from anxiety is to engage his mind in undisturbing things. Usually varied experiences are more effective in diverting the mind than is a uniform experience. Varied experiences, therefore, not only give pleasure; they also free the mind from disturbances.

This book is divided into three parts: Part One pertains to dealing with people in life situations in general; Part Two, to preventing unwholesome behavior due to tedium; Part Three, to furthering mental health. In Part One the importance of varying our behavior so as to interest other persons in us is emphasized and methods of procedure are discussed. Parts Two and Three are devoted to methods of arranging and managing human affairs so that variety may be had by those who participate in them. The entire volume also suggests how a person may obtain variety for his own enjoyment.

PART ONE

DEALING WITH PEOPLE IN LIFE SITUATIONS
IN GENERAL

CHAPTER I

EXPRESSING VARIED THOUGHTS AND ATTITUDES

A PERSON holds attention and gives pleasure when from his lips or pen new ideas come as soon as his hearer or reader is ready for change. Many people make a strong impression and give enjoyment because what they say presents a varied picture. The one who imparts interesting ideas is always refreshing. Anyone who, on the other hand, dwells excessively on a single thought or reverts to it again and again grows stale; he cannot long be interesting who fiddles on one string. The person who talks sex, shop or politics may be rebuffed not because of a dislike for his subject, but because he talks of it continually. Faded talk is more unpleasant than monotonous work. Why? Because when a person is engaged in a routine occupation he can leave the task to his hands and go wandering mentally, but when in the presence of a man of narrow mental range it is usually necessary at least to appear attentive to what he says in order to avoid offending him. Through the ages people have cried out against talk and writing that consist in the repeated showing of the same thing, and have delighted in accompanying the person whose words present a diversified picture. The following couplet in regard to writing is equally applicable to what one says in speech.

"Tire not too long one subject when you write,
'tis variety that gives delight."[1]

Thoughts differ in degree of unusualness, and most highly novel thoughts are very refreshing. Original thought, whether new in subject matter or simply in point of view, may stand out from other discourse like a rainbow in the sky. People who say new things are often sought out and enjoyed. Whether or not their words make a lasting impression depends, of course, on the soundness of what they say.

It takes a fertile brain to produce good thought, but there are persons who have sound original ideas that they do not express. An individual who lacks distinction for being a creative thinker sometimes gets a new idea but dismisses it as worthless simply on the ground that it is his own; or he may feel confident that his idea has merit, but lacks the courage to present it. Later he may find his own rejected thought stated by someone else. Great works frequently present what was often thought, but never before expressed. Hesitancy in presenting a good original idea may, instead of resulting in someone else presenting it, result in what is worse, the loss of the idea. Persons who are most justified in expressing their thoughts are often most reticent. More self-confidence on the part of able minds would add richness to human relationships. So, if you have a light, for the sake of yourself and for the good of all, do not keep it under a bushel.

When sound original ideas cannot be produced, it is

[1] Vida, Marco Girolamo. *Art of Poetry*, Bk. 2, l. 218. See Albert S. Cook, *The Art of Poetry*, p. 91. New York, G. E. Stechert and Company, 1926.

possible to express unusual thought for the sake of amusement by saying what one does not mean, provided one is not taken seriously. No matter what the nonsense, if it is new and presented in a light vein it will amuse. Unsound but playful original thought furnishes much amusement in various social situations, and a sense of humor is, in part, the ability to say and to take the extraordinary in a light vein.

Information and news, like original thought, may be enjoyed for their unusualness. The novelty of information and news is always a factor in the attention it arouses and in the pleasure it gives. Whether one tells of an extraordinary thing or of an extraordinary interpretation of a commonplace, the effect is the same; the mind of the listener is made eager and harkens to what is said. The more anything differs from what is customary, the greater is the interest it excites. Such facts as those reported in the *National Geographic Magazine* and in newspapers owe their appeal primarily to their unusual nature. News may also be stirring in character, and so provide not only new thoughts but also new emotional experiences. Hearing or reading about a great disaster that befell others breaks the humdrum for many persons by putting them through sudden and pronounced changes in thinking and feeling. News of a river overflowing its banks and sweeping whole towns into its channel gives countless thousands release from the tedium of their customary thoughts and feelings, and renews interest in human relationships by providing material for conversation.

It is not simply the change of thought and feeling, but also the realization of having escaped harm oneself that gives satisfaction when learning of a disaster that befell another person. As Lucretius said, " 'Tis sweet, when the seas are tossed by violent winds, to view from land the toils of others, not that there is pleasure in seeing others in distress, but that man is glad to know himself secure."

It is possible to be sympathetic with persons in distress and at the same time enjoy the excitement and the feeling of being secure that result from knowing of their misfortune. But there are degrees of sympathy, and, of course, those who are enlivened and elated more than they are distressed by the adversity of others have little sympathetic feeling for them.

Overstatements of fact, like original thought, information and news, may be enjoyed because of the unusualness they express. A father and his son once ran a footrace down a lane, and when they came to the end the boy said, "You beat me all right, but look how you puff!" The father replied, "The reason you don't puff as much as I do is that you're too tired to puff." Tall men have been asked, "How's the air up there," and statements, such as the following are common: *About a million were present. It was so hot you could fry eggs in the sun. You could see it grow. It smelled to high heaven. The wind goes right through you. You could hear the explosion a thousand miles away. It was more delectable than the nectar of the gods. The air was so thick you could cut it with a knife. The earth trembles with the tread of armies.*

Fiction, likewise, is often enjoyed because of the unusualness of which it tells. Tales of adventure involving struggle with uncivilized man, with beasts of the jungles or with giant sea monsters are enjoyed because they are amazing, and when such tales contain animals or human beings that have unusual names they are especially captivating to children. Stories of the supernatural, involving fairies, ghosts and witches, have astounded with delight people of all ages. So great is the interest in the unusual that tales always grow in the telling.

In relating a story to an extremely sensitive person, care must be taken to avoid giving the impression that one intends him to take the story as something that actually happened. A story-teller should indicate to such a person, in one way or another, that he does not expect to be taken seriously, or should tell a story that is such an obvious exaggeration or misrepresentation of fact that there can be no question as to whether he expects it to be believed. Such precautions are necessary to keep the sensitive listener from thinking that he is considered stupid enough to believe the story.

Some people tell stories as personal experiences, rather than as accounts of events in which they did not play a part. My dentist has the knack of amusing children while working on their teeth by telling them of his adventures in Africa. He even shows them ivory in his cabinet that came from the tusks of an elephant he killed. The children know that what he says isn't true, but they enjoy listening to the accounts of his hairbreadth escapes and triumphs. Recently there has been a flare-up of liars' clubs in which a prize is given to the one who can tell the tallest tale about himself. We like to hear things we can't believe because we like the unusual. And when a story-teller involves himself, he gives the tale a personal touch which makes it more amusing.

Although interest in the unusualness of a thought is

often very great, interest in thought itself is more fundamental, and people differ much in what they like to hear or read. Anyone who speaks or writes is a bore unless people are interested in what he says. Every change of subject must, therefore, be carefully made.

To be interesting, a person who makes pretense of saying something must say it. Delay in coming to the point gives the mind nothing and keeps it from wandering to fields of its own. It is pleasant to be with someone who does not bore and irritate you in this way. Once upon a time there was such a man. In his talk and writing he never delayed saying what he set out to say. He was welcome wherever he went, and was urged sincerely to come oftener and to stay longer. This man's name was Jones, and he was known as the man who doesn't bore anyone. Never did he hesitate much in speech, and never did he clog the main stream of thought with insufferable details. At no time did he check the flow of thought with such ponderings and digressions as, "I think it was on the twenty-sixth of April—no, it couldn't have been then because. . . . Perhaps it was on the . . . but I'm not sure of that. I don't know what's wrong with my memory. But, whenever it was, the date doesn't matter. As I was saying . . ." Never did anyone need to hurry this man along with such questions as, "What happened after that?", "How did it finally come out?" When he was asked a pointed question, he always answered; he never said, "I'm coming to that." This man who never bored anyone also had the delightful quality of being able to talk on a subject without often pausing to give his attention to something else, or simply to think or to rest his mind. Mr. Jones moreover always talked in a sufficiently audible tone to make it unnecessary to call and wait for a repetition of what he said, and he could answer a question without giving a speech. Talk that moves duly from point to point and that omits unwanted details never bores.

To be pleasing, serious talk or writing must take a definite course and express related thought, rather than shift aimlessly and convey disconnected ideas. We like to see things that are put together fit together. Connected thought of a weighty character is preferred to the disconnected also because relationships seen between ideas add to their significance and make retention easier. Carrying on conversation along a definite course is also more complimentary to one's companion than random talk, because it gives the companion the impression of being satisfied with what he says. Related talk is also easy to follow; unrelated talk, difficult to follow and fatiguing.

"There are men of esprit who are excessively exhausting to some people. They are the talkers who have what may be called *jerky* minds. Their thoughts do not run in the natural order of sequence. They say bright things on all possible subjects, but their zigzags rack you to death. After a jolting half-hour with one of these jerky companions, talking with a dull friend affords relief. It is like taking a cat in your lap after holding a squirrel." [2]

Although serious talk, to be appreciated, must usually take a definite course, it need not be restricted to a single part of a subject. Usually the more varied the phases of a subject treated, the more interesting the discourse.

[2] Holmes, Oliver Wendell. *The Autocrat of the Breakfast-Table*, Essay 1.

Change from one phase of a subject to another, however serious the nature of the subject, is often as refreshing as a change of scene.

In discourse intended to be carried on in a light vein, the boundaries of subjects should be disregarded; talk should touch upon everything and concentrate on nothing. This is because no one can dwell long on a subject without growing serious about it, especially when one meets opposition. There are different occasions that justify light talk. Some social functions are intended to give play to the sprightly feelings; they are intended for recreation. On such occasions serious talk on any of the subjects of the day is out of order. On some occasions persons who hold opposite views on certain subjects and who are highly emotional and wholly unalterable in their views are brought together. It is then prudent to do no more than skirt controversial subjects in a playful manner.

In their zeal to say something that is of interest to another person, some maintain silence and so develop anxiety which interferes with thought. It is never so difficult to speak as when one is embarrassed by one's silence, and the longer talk has been suspended, the harder it is to find something to say. Rather than create a pause that is paralyzing, one should say something, anything, no matter how banal, to which one's companion can make reply. A remark, however trite, that breaks the silence is always received better than a pause when those in one's presence are interested in conversation.

Although it is possible to give much enjoyment by keeping up a flow of thoughts, one fails to please by a continuous outpouring. This is because unremitting talk tends to grow monotonous and because it keeps the hearer from having other thoughts to which he may prefer to devote his mind. One reason people sometimes like to go alone to a shopping center, for a walk, or on a long journey, is that when doing so they can view and think what they wish without being interrupted with questions, remarks, or with requests to look here or to look there. Talking too much is as bad as or worse than talking too little. It is always wise for a person to consider the possibility of pleasing another by affording him change from hearing one talk to thinking his own thoughts. But a person must be silent with discretion; there is a time for speech and a time for silence, and one must be silent in season.

The interest people take in an idea expressed is determined not only by what is said, but also by their attitude toward the one who says it. The most unusual thought can be made stale by the channel through which it flows. There are persons so disliked that every subject they touch turns at once into an uninteresting one. If people like you, everything you say is interesting; if they do not like you, nothing you say is interesting. The problem of pleasing people, therefore, involves more than the presentation of interesting ideas; it involves also the building up of good will.

Because of either personal inadequacy or lack of common interest, it is often difficult to occupy the mind sufficiently through conversation alone. This is a reason why people in getting together engage in activity, such as playing cards or hiking, or have music as a background for conversation at a dinner. Arrangements of these kinds serve not only to fill the time that is not occupied by conversation, but also to prevent uninteresting talk, which a lack of something to do may force. The supplementing of conversation with other things has, of course, disadvantages. The card player who is interested in the game and the card player who is interested in conversation are sure to clash; the speaking voice does not blend well with musical notes, and it is difficult to converse against the sound of music. But the practice of supplementing talk with other activity or amusement often serves the purpose of keeping the mind engaged in interesting ways. Even when having very congenial conversation we often desire to engage in additional activity.

The need for aiding conversation by keeping the mind occupied with an additional experience is, however, not always as great as it is assumed to be. A person's talk often founders not because of a lack of something to say, but because of the attitude of his company. It is remarkable how our wits are affected by the company we are in. There are people who stimulate our minds and there are others who paralyze them. When you find another person inarticulate, it is always well to consider the possibility of being responsible for his silence, and, if responsible, to create an atmosphere that will enable him to become articulate.

To be interesting, it is necessary to be varied in attitude, as well as in thought. A person who can be lively or calm, jocular or serious, or otherwise variable in attitude in accordance with the situation soon finds his presence felt and enjoyed. The one who, on the other hand, is always in the same mood is as monotonous as the person who has but few ideas. Even the most cherished attitudes can be prolonged to such an extent that they become wearisome. Although such tragedies are rare, it is possible to kill another person with kindness.

The thoughts and attitudes that most people express are more monotonous than those they actually possess. This is because they do not say what they think nor act as they feel. Many people are monotonous in thought or attitude because they aim to conform entirely to certain ideals of their own or of the group. Such persons may try always to smile or never to smile. Those who do little more than echo the common thought bore others and are bored by them. Extreme conventionality begets much dreariness.

Some persons are monotonous in attitude because they yield invariably to the views of others—because they respond as does a looking-glass. Such persons are, moreover, responsible for much monotony on the part of others because disagreement is sometimes necessary to make conversation flow. Dissent, and sometimes friendly belligerency, underlies some of the most spirited discussions. Kites rise against the wind. But there are many persons whose feelings are hurt by even very modest disagreement. When dealing with such persons it is often expedient to refrain from taking issue with what they say. The need of reticence in disagreeing with another person's idea depends much on whether he desires approval or the stimulation of an opposite view. To some, continual agreement is boresome; to others, it is elating. The restraint to be exercised in objecting to another's view depends, however, not only on that person, but also on the manner in which one objects to his view. Disagreement is refreshing when expressed in the spirit of finding out truth; wretched when expressed only to prove another wrong. There are many ways of disagreeing without being disagreeable.[3]

Just as there are persons who are monotonous because they yield invariably to one's view, there are others who are monotonous because they dissent regularly from it. Some oppose everything that is said because in this way they obtain feelings of importance. Others do so because they feel antagonistic toward those whose ideas they oppose. "There's one rule I've been guided by, in settlin' how to vote, allers,—I take the side that is n't took by them consarned teetotallers."[4] The negativistic person is as monotonous as is the one who always says, "Yes."

Variety of expression should be attained only within the limits of individuality; one should always remain oneself. The person who expresses himself independently of the thoughts and attitudes of others has a certain distinctiveness. He contrasts markedly with the society of which he is a part. His individuality may make him liked by many people. The one who, on the other hand, is all types of character by fits and starts and no type long usually fails to please because he is nobody in particular. Such a person may attract others at first, but he invariably disappoints them later because of having apparently undergone a change of character. To be thought of as a distinct human being everyone must have something in his way of thinking and acting that characterizes him. But individuality in itself does not necessarily make one attractive. There are persons who have unpleasant idio-

[3] See Wendell White, *The Psychology of Dealing with People*, Ch. V. New York, The Macmillan Company, 1936.
[4] Lowell, James Russell. *The Biglow Papers*, No. IX.

syncrasies; others who are too individualistic to get along with anyone. A woman whose husband was such a character said that when her boy grows up she is going to have him join a fraternity so that he will become like others. The most pleasing individuality usually results not from striving to develop distinguishing characteristics, but simply from expressing oneself sincerely.

Thus to get attention and to make ourselves interesting to other persons we must be well-varied in thought and attitude.

CHAPTER II

EXPRESSING THOUGHTS IN VARIED WAYS

THOUGHTS that are stated again and again in the same language often appear tarnished, but by expressing them in new ways one restores their luster. The repetition of thought is, of course, sometimes as worthy an aim in expression as avoidance of repetition is at other times. The presenting of an idea repeatedly may be justified because that idea brings pleasure, or because instruction or persuasion requires repetition. But any idea makes a deeper impression and gives more pleasure if it comes, from time to time, in different garbs. Repeat some ideas often, but not always in the same language. There are many dresses for thought and more can be made that are equally acceptable. It is possible to express an idea for the hundredth time and yet be original in doing so. For instance, the following question has been raised often, but presumably never before in this way: *Should I provide for the old man that I am to become, or spend what I have and let him take care of himself?* Talk that fascinates and pages that traverse seas usually involve strokes of invention in manner of expression. Speech or writing that, on the other hand, goes unheeded does not necessarily lack substance; frequently it merely fails to rise above the dead level of monotony of expression. In speaking to be heard and in writing to be read it is always well to consider the possibility of phrasing thought in varied ways.

Precision of expression itself prevents monotony of language. It is possible to convey many slightly different ideas loosely by the same word or phrase, but to say exactly what one has in mind necessitates the use of separate terms for ideas that have a shade of difference in meaning. The person who states his thoughts with real precision will, therefore, of necessity use to some extent varied language. But saying exactly what one has in mind does not necessarily give the diversity to language that the art of speech or writing demands. Frequently there is an expression that conveys thought accurately but which is so hackneyed that it displeases the ear or the eye. As successful speakers and writers know, one may be clear without being interesting. "The sufficient word does not suffice." Diversity, as well as precision of language, is, therefore, needed. There are many ways of giving variety to the expression of thought.

1. Using a Variety of Words

Although precision of expression usually requires the use of one particular term, it often permits a choice from among several words. It is well, therefore, when repeating the same idea in successive sentences to avoid, to some extent, the employment of the same term with noticeable frequency; to use synonymous terms when precision permits. Likewise, when repeating a remark from time to time, as is frequently done, a change in terms used is pleasant to hear. The card player who still asks, "Who dealt this mess?" imposes on the good nature of the other players.

Of the available words for the expression of thought, some are newer than others. And the use of a variety of the newer words usually makes discourse more interesting than does the use of a variety of hackneyed terms. In conveying familiar thought, it is often very important to express it by means of the more novel words; words that make the familiar thought new.

On the other hand, in our emphasis on the striking and pleasing stylistic effect of novel language, we must not overlook the value of familiar expressions. Common words that have not been used too widely often make meaning clear, and clearness is the basic principle of expression. Familiar terms also seem more sincere than novel expressions. They have a frankness about them that makes people take what they say in good faith, as they would a gold coin of a known stamp. Everyday expressions are so characteristic of honesty of purpose that they are often taken for honesty. Simplicity of language, furthermore, conveys the notion that the speaker or writer understands what he says, for it is a well-known fact that the more we become masters of our subject matter, the more simply we can express it. Statements that are over the heads of others are sometimes also over the head of the speaker or writer. Familiar terms are superior to novel expressions, especially for stirring the heart. Ideas that people hold dear become definitely associated with their customary dress. Many a familiar term at once gives rise to a rich array of fond memories. The word *birthplace* may enable the one on whose ears it falls to visualize a thousand of his childhood doings. The influence of common terms over the heart is particularly great in highly personal relationships. Familiar words alone can be intimate and dear. To move the heart it is necessary to call a thing by its own name.

Although a novel term is often less clear than a familiar term, less apparently sincere, less suggestive of understanding, or less capable of moving the heart, it serves a purpose that the common term cannot serve—that of giving occasionally the thrill of something new. The novel expression can say to the familiar expression, as the squirrel said to the mountain, "If I cannot carry heavy forests on my back, neither can you crack a nut." [1]

To give novelty to expression, a term need not be new; it need only be used in a new context. Although "interesting" is a common word, it gives novelty to the title of this book *The Psychology of Making Life Interesting*, because it is unfamiliar and different from the hundreds of "success" book-titles that have appeared.

Variety in the use of words is attainable through the use of slang. May a person use slang? One kind of slang is invented to express ideas incapable of expression in the standard language. May one use slang to convey thought for which there is no other adequate expression? It would be absurd to object to the use of slang in such cases. Until recently *publicize* and *jazz* were slang terms for which there was no equivalent word in the standard language. Their use was, therefore, justified. The word "chisel" used to designate the employment of shrewd or unfair methods for attaining some selfish end may, although it is a slang term, be justified for the same reason. Slang for which there is no other adequate expression is, however, very uncommon because seldom does anyone

[1] Emerson, Ralph Waldo. From "Fable."

find the standard language inadequate for the expression of his thoughts and feelings.

A more common type of slang consists of old words mutilated or misapplied and of new words invented for the pleasure of novelty. A widely known illustration of a mutilated word is *all righty* for *all right;* of a misapplied word is *park*, used as a verb in reference to leaving an article temporarily, or remaining personally for a short time in a certain place. Slang of either of these two types is often picked up by many persons because it is unusual. It is picked up also, and with equal readiness, for the pleasure of being in the fashion. Slang for which there is an equivalent in the standard lanaguage should never be used in serious speech or writing. This is primarily because unless an addition to the language is justified to convey thought it is unjustified. The unnecessary use of slang in serious speech or writing is objectionable also because when a person uses such slang he may give the impression of being in a trifling mood, rather than in a serious state of mind. And lack of seriousness is out of keeping with formal discourse. The use of such slang might also give the impression that one is ignorant of the language. Slang for which there is an equivalent in the standard language may, however, be used when speaking in a light vein. Its use at such times is not regarded as an indication of ignorance of the language, and it is in harmony with the occasion. But much slang that the individual uses when he is in a flippant mood is vivid, and may, therefore, soon be employed so widely that it becomes commonplace. The vivid nature of slang also makes the repeated use of it noticeable. For these reasons slang must always be used with discretion lest it become montonous, and so defeat the purpose for which it is intended. It is usually only by being among the first to use a slang expression and by employing that expression sparingly that one can be colorful in using it.

Good coined terms are rare, and, therefore, are especially striking. The principles governing the coining of words are similar to those governing the use of slang. One may coin a word for conveying thought for which there is no other suitable expression. However, a person so infrequently finds the established language inadequate for conveying thought that the coining of words for precision of expression is seldom justified. Words may be coined on playful occasions for the pleasure of novelty. But to be received with favor an invented word must be very apt.

2. *Varying One's Sentence Structure*

Variety in the structure of sentences is involved in all pleasing forms of expression. In what ways can a person vary his sentence structure? Most sentences are declarative sentences. It is possible, therefore, to achieve interesting variety by using sometimes an exclamatory sentence; sometimes an imperative sentence, such as, *Doubt the man who swears to his devotion;* by using sometimes a rhetorical question—a question that one asks without expecting a reply, such as the second sentence in this paragraph. The question is of value not only because it adds variety to sentence structure, but also because it gives the hearer or reader a feeling of being in close communication with the speaker or writer. Variety of discourse can also be attained by a conscious alternation of simple, complex, compound and complex-compound sentences. Another way of varying sentence structure in speech or writing is to make sentences different in length. The long sentence in which the oath of office is usually administered to the person being installed into that office and the brief reply, "I do," although not purposely made to contrast, are interesting because they do so. Variety can be produced also by *transposition*. Transposition is the rearranging of sentence structure from the usual English pattern. This pattern is as follows: adjectives modifying the subject, subject, adjective phrase or clause, verb, adverb, or adverbial phrase or clause, and object or other complement with its modifiers. Any change in this order, such as the changes below, may be pleasing because of the variety it affords.

Sentences Beginning with a Verb
"Came the dawn."
"Said Mr. Smith in the conclusion of his address . . ."

Sentences Beginning with an Adverb
"Often we make a person pay dearly for what we give him."
"Swiftly flies each tale of shame or folly."

Sentences Beginning with Predicate Adjectives
"Great is work which lends dignity to man."
"Correct you are."

Sentences Beginning with an Infinitive
"To enjoy a thing exclusively is commonly to exclude yourself from the true enjoyment of it."
"To be confident of pleasing others is often an infallible means of displeasing."

Sentences Beginning with Dependent Clauses
"When one is emotional, the mind abdicates."
"If you want friends, let others occasionally gain ascendency over you."

An occasional change in the usual order of the parts of a sentence not only gives variety, but also centers the mind on the element out of the usual position, and so serves to emphasize it. Transposition is most natural when a person is moved by strong feeling. Frequent or forced use of it is, therefore, likely to give the impression of artificiality.

A pleasing effect can sometimes be produced by a number of similar sentences in succession. After reading a number of sentences that are varied in structure, such as the preceding sentences of this chapter, one finds a number of highly similar sentences, such as those in the following two quotations, as striking as persons seen in uniform against a background of a number of people in ordinary dress.

"When, in America, the world's most productive grassland becomes a desert on the march and casts its dusty shadow nearly 2,000 miles to the Atlantic ocean, we know that something is amiss. When the fertile farms of American midlands slide silently layer by layer downstream to build mud flats on the floor of the Gulf of Mexico, we become worried. When magnificent forests dwindle to burned-over wastes of blackened stumps incapable of restocking themselves in timber, . . . our fear deepens to alarm." [2]

"It was women as well as men who were scandalized at the idea of taxing the public to maintain public schools for the education of 'She's.' It was women who regarded the high school, the college and the university education as indelicate for women. It was women who refused to speak to Dr. Elizabeth Blackwell, the first woman physician. It was women who cried shame at Susan B. Anthony when she arose to address a teachers' convention in the state of New York. It was

[2] Renner, George T. "Human Ecology—A New Social Science," *Teachers College Record*, p. 483 (May 1938).

women who cried 'served them right' when several of the leading newspapers of the country editorially stigmatized the first women who attempted to speak in public as 'she hyenas.' It was wives, when the first petition to the legislature for property rights for women was circulated, who refused to sign it upon the ground that the control of property was the just privilege of husbands." [3]

Sentences whose parts are similar—sentences that have *balanced construction*—are also interesting because such sentences are uncommon. Note the sentences:

"He who receives a good turn should never forget it; he who does a good turn should never remember it."

"The more you speak of yourself, the more you are likely to lie."

"The tone of good conversation is brilliant and natural.—It is neither tedious nor frivolous.—It is instructive without pedantry; gay, without tumultuousness; polished, without insipidity; waggish, without equivocation."

"Desultory studies are erased from the mind as easily as pencil marks; classified studies are retained like durable ink."

Repetition of the same sound at the beginning of two or more words immediately succeeding each other or at short intervals—*alliteration*—is likewise interesting because it is uncommon. Note Benjamin Franklin's admonition: "Waste not, want not; willful waste makes woeful want."

A person can achieve a variety of sentences, just as he can achieve a variety of words, by expressing himself with precision; and a skillful adaptation of form to matter is the first means whereby one should endeavor to

[3] Catt, Carrie Chapman. "Woman Suffrage Must Win," *Independent*, Vol. 84, p. 56 (October 11, 1915).

vary the form of his sentences. The desired amount of diversity in sentence structure is, however, attained only through conscious effort toward its attainment.

The effectiveness of a sentence is, of course, due not simply to the fact that it gives variety; its effectiveness may be due primarily to the attractiveness of its structure or to what the sentence says. The attractiveness of the sentences used as examples here and in other chapters must, therefore, be regarded as due to various factors in addition to the principles that they illustrate.

3. Expressing Ideas in Contrast with Each Other

Contrast is dissimilitude of associated things. Opposites attract attention because they are different from each other, and, in many cases, because one of the opposites is distinctly different from what is customary. The most prosaic thing is made less prosaic when it is set off by its opposite. In addition to giving diversity to the mind, contrast also makes meaning clear, for a thing is best understood when it is thought of in relation to its opposite. Contrast produces such a striking effect and makes points stand out so clearly that one should make it a rule never to engage in extended expression without considering the possibility of providing contrast. The following quotations serve as illustrations.

"The propagandist is one who, instead of opening minds, closes them."

"Man was born free, but everywhere he is in chains."

"Good writing is not simply that which can be understood, but that which cannot be misunderstood."

"Men may come and men may go,
But I go on forever."

"A specialist is one who strives to learn more and more about less and less."

"In our personal ambitions we are individualists. But in our seeking for economic and political progress as a nation, we all go up—or else we all go down—as a people."

"This country cannot endure permanently half free and half slave."

"There are many people who delight most in what they least understand."

"This country will not be a good place for any of us to live in unless we make it a good place for all of us to live in."

"He waved the olive branch with an iron fist."

"Oft was thought, but ne'er so well expressed."

"And those who came to scoff remained to pray."

"Keep your eyes wide open when you are looking for a mate, but half closed after marriage."

"Good interest is bad security."

"The best way to do good to ourselves, is to do it to others; the right way to gather is to scatter."

"We rise in glory as we sink in pride."

"A home that cost three million dollars and a breakfast that cost five thousand are disquieting facts to the millions who live in a hut and dine on a crust. The fact that a man . . . has an income of twenty million dollars falls strangely on the ears of those who hear it as they sit empty-handed with children crying for bread."

The production of contrast is a main guiding principle of the dramatist in selecting and shaping material. In every kind of dramatic composition, whether intended to be acted or read, opposites are set up against each other. As Leo Zachary says, "No contrast, no drama." Dramatic works present all sorts of people, and each of the principal characters portrayed is distinctly different from another. On the stage or on the printed page there may appear the practical-minded and the dreamer, the loyal and the unfaithful, the level-headed and the irrational, the narrow-minded and the liberal, the humane and the beastly, the sympathetic and the indifferent, the worldly wise and the unsophisticated, homely folks and society dowagers, opposite sexes, or the masculine and the effeminate of the same sex. Frequently the contrast in drama is between two parts of a man's nature. A character may have bold words and cowardly action, or may have youth and the dignity of a mature man. In many dramatic works, sudden and pronounced change of scene occurs; in some, a scene of gaiety is abruptly ended and succeeded by a scene of horror and grief. The same is true in many stories. Whittier's *Snow Bound* presents harsh elements of nature outside of the home, and comfort within. The relaxation suggested by the abundance of provisions, by the simple and congenial activity of the people and by the dog stretched out before the fire marks a sharp contrast with the forbidding exterior.

4. *Proceeding with One's Subject in Different Ways*

There are ideas that need to be presented again and again. But few ideas can be presented often in the same way without their repetition becoming tedious. An idea may, however, be repeated interestingly by presenting it from time to time in different ways. It may be presented first as a general principle, and then a number of times by means of illustrations. The preceding treatment of the subject of contrast suggests the extent to which the central idea of one's discourse may be repeated by means of illustrations without the repetition becoming monotonous. The chief purpose of illustrations is, of course, to clarify thought. They sometimes remove a veil of obscurity that can be removed in no other way. But the fact that illustrations give variety only incidentally to serving their main purpose of clarifying thought does not limit their value for varying one's discourse.

An idea can be repeated interestingly also by giving statistics and by making comparisons. In the development of the idea that education costs are not excessive, a writer said, "However highly we may rate the service rendered to the nation by the life insurance business, the question may be raised whether it is any more important than the service rendered by public education. The fact is that at present we are spending $1.35 for life insurance for each $1.00 spent for public schools."

A person may attain variety in the presentation of his subject also by telling a story, by reasoning with an individual or a group, by illustrating with lantern slides, or by quoting other persons. A speaker or writer who by means of quotations has other persons take part in the presentation of his subject is more varied in style than is the one who presents his subject wholly by himself. A quotation makes style especially colorful if its language is uncommon, and many successful speakers and writers use such quotations. In emphasizing the need of repetition in public address a speaker told the story of a colored preacher who, when asked to account for his success as a preacher, said, "First I tells 'em what I's gwine to tell 'em. Then I tells 'em. Then I tells 'em what I's done told 'em." The unusualness of the language of the familiar couplet of Robert Burns, given below, likewise adds to the interest in the thought it expresses.

"O wad some Power the giftie gie us
To see oursels as ithers see us."

Although a quotation often constitutes a very pleasing change from one's own words, it is easy to quote excessively. Too frequent reference to the words of others is as monotonous as is language that is restricted to the words of the speaker or writer, and suggests timidity and a lack of originality. But a fitting quotation often creates as much interest as does any other means of varying one's discourse.

5. Arousing Mental Pictures of Several Senses

The novice in speech or writing is often monotonous because he tells only what he sees; the artist is interesting because he tells also what he hears, feels, smells or tastes. In describing the trees of a forest, Thomas Hardy gives more auditory than visual pictures.

"To dwellers in a wood, almost every species of tree has its voice as well as its feature. At the passing of the breeze, the fir-trees sob and moan no less distinctly than they rock; the holly whistles as it battles with itself; the ash hisses amid its quiverings; the beech rustles while its flat boughs rise and fall. And winter, which modifies the note of such trees as shed their leaves, does not destroy its individuality."

The following words from Robert Ingersoll's Indianapolis address of 1876 also give auditory as well as visual images. Note that they contain two auditory images of stillness.

"As we cover the graves of the heroic dead with flowers, the past rises before us like a dream. Again we are in the great struggle for national life. We hear the sounds of preparation

—the music of boisterous drums—the silver voices of heroic bugles. We hear the appeals of orators; we see the pale cheeks of women, and the flushed faces of men; we see all the dead whose dust we have covered with flowers. We lose sight of them no more. We are with them when they enlist in the great army of freedom. We see them part from those they love. Some are walking for the last time in the quiet woody places with the maidens they adore. We hear the whispers and the sweet vows of eternal love as they lingeringly part forever. Others are bending over cradles kissing babies that are asleep. Some are receiving the blessings of old men. Some are parting from mothers who hold them and press them to their hearts again and again and say nothing. And some are talking with wives and trying with brave words spoken in the old tones to drive from their hearts the awful fear. We see them part. We see the wife standing in the door with the babe in her arms—standing in the sunlight sobbing; at the turn of the road a hand waves—she answers by holding high in her loving arms the child. He is gone and forever."

In explaining why people like to witness fires, a person can give images of every sense. In trying to do so, one might write as follows:

"Few things are more sensational than a fire. Madly leaping and glowing flames, flying sparks, belching smoke, the crackling of burning timber, scorching heat, shrieking fire engines, water that spouts and that chills the bystander with icy sprays, the odor of burning materials, smothering fumes, crumbling walls, and jostling crowds make fire exciting."

Although expression that brings to mind various images is more interesting than that which gives images of but one sense, most of what we say is of necessity primarily visual or auditory, because most of our actual experiences are chiefly of either or both of these types. The infrequency of expression that arouses other sensory images, however, makes them very striking, and so one should not overlook opportunity to employ them.

Frequently it is difficult to present an idea in the form of a mental picture by the use of direct language. But a corresponding idea suggestive of the idea you wish to convey can always be presented in the form of a mental picture of various senses through the use of figures of speech. Note the following illustrations.

"An instructor, observing that a student was arousing the disfavor of the class by participating too much in discussions, called the student's attention to this privately, and added, 'It might be well for you to swim under water for a while.'"

"In paying tribute to a member of a group the speaker said, 'He is the kind of a man that likes to see your ship come to shore, and when his own capsizes he still wants yours to sail safely to port.'"

"That man's the true Conservative
Who lops the molded branch away."

"There can be no peace in this world until we learn to use the brakes—as well as the horns of our cars."

Figures of speech not only give imagery; they also constitute means of expression in addition to plain or ordinary means, and so give scope to what would be without their use a scanty tongue. No one adept in the use of figurative language need overwork a standard term; no such a person ever need become monotonous.

In addition to being interesting because of the variety they afford, figures of speech make easier the expression of thought; they enable one to define the otherwise undefinable. They also further apprehension. Frequently there is difficulty in getting the individual to understand an idea that has been well stated in a literal way. But a figure used in the presentation of an idea often illuminates that idea sufficiently to make apprehension easy.

Whether using direct language or figures of speech, one can arouse images of several senses by a single word. The first of each pair of words below arouses only one type of imagery; the second, more than one type.

Words	Senses Appealed to
soft	touch
cottony	touch and sight
white	sight
snowy	sight and temperature
closed	sight
slammed	sight and sound
weep	sight
sob	sight, hearing and movement
gray	sight
leaden	sight and pressure
cut	sight
chop	sight, hearing and movement

It is apparent that the second of each of these pairs of words (which arouses images of several senses) is more interesting than is the first (which arouses but one image). Speech or writing in which a single word gives images of several senses is not apt to be monotonous.

Mental pictures may be aroused directly or indirectly. They are aroused directly by the use of words that represent them. All of the above examples of arousing images are examples of the direct method. The indirect method of arousing a mental picture of something consists in simply telling of the effect of a person or thing upon the observer. The hearer or reader, upon learning of the impression produced by something, may call up in imagination a picture of that person or thing. Different individuals get in this way different mental pictures, but that fact may serve rather than hinder the purpose of the speaker or writer. Homer, in trying to make Helen of Troy appear attractive in his story of the Trojan war, might have given a literal description of her; but nothing that he could have said would have made her seem attractive to all of his readers of his age or of future ages. He, however, gave his imaginative readers a picture of her by the indirect method, and with an effectiveness that makes her rise in their minds with all conceivable charm. He wrote, in substance, that an old man in Troy, who had never seen Helen, said to another old man while they were sitting on a wall waiting for the king and Helen to pass, "It's a disgrace to fight a war like this for that woman. Think of all the fine young men that are being killed over her. What we should do is pack up the wench and send her home." Just then the king and Helen of Troy came into view. Instantly this same old man exclaimed, "Look! Is that Helen? Say—this war is going on!" Thus Homer molded Helen of Troy into every imaginative reader's ideal. One more illustration is sufficient to make clear the possibility of arousing mental pictures indirectly. "But as it is written, Eye hath not seen, nor ear heard, neither have entered into the heart of man, the things which God prepared for them that love him." In the mind of an imaginative person, this passage should create a heaven more glorious than words could describe.

6. *Expressing Oneself with a Silent Look*

Talking involves normally the voice and play of the features. Expression of thought by means of the features alone is, therefore, unusual. Because of its novelty, the language of the countenance alone often accomplishes the purpose of speech more effectively than would be possible by a combination of verbal and physical expression. But the effectiveness of a look unaccompanied by words is due not only to the novelty of such expression, but also to the fact that to be speechless implies that a person has feelings too deep or too stirring for words. A speechless look may, therefore, be sweeter than words, sharper than words, or more persuasive than words; may be the most eloquent form of expression.

Means in addition to those considered in this chapter for giving variety to one's manner of expression consist in arousing curiosity, creating suspense, and giving surprise. Because these techniques deserve extended treatment, the following three chapters will be devoted to them.

CHAPTER III

AROUSING CURIOSITY

Curiosity is an inquisitive attitude created by the unfamiliarity of that which is the object of attention or thought, and so arousing curiosity consists in creating expectation of something unusual. In doing so one stimulates interest effectively. Curiosity involves an emotional state, as well as an inquiring mind, and so provides change of emotion, as well as change of thought. A state of curiosity is invigorating—it gives one a sense of being alive, which makes it enjoyable for its own sake, as well as for the change of experience it gives.

In addition to being pleasurable, curiosity arouses activity. Children forever ask questions regarding anything new, and have ready fingers to touch and manipulate the unfamiliar. Grownups, similarly, are eager to be informed regarding things of a novel character. Curiosity has tempted many from the comforts of home and has led them to strange and hazardous regions, and many more it has kept in libraries, in laboratories or in consultation with persons informed on subjects of interest to them.

"Ah, Curiosity! by thee inspired
The truth to know how oft has man inquired!" [1]

[1] Sprague, Charles. From "Curiosity." See Rufus Wilmot Griswold, *The Poets and Poetry of America*. Philadelphia, Carey and Hart, 1842.

In his inquisitiveness man is not unlike the beasts and birds that circle around anything new, eying it or sniffing it. But man, because of his extensive mental life, is curious about infinitely more things than are animals.

Examples of the use of curiosity-provoking techniques in influencing behavior may be observed on every hand. In trying to get the public interested in a talk that lacks immediate appeal, the promoters usually make only a general statement as to the speaker's subject. Curiosity thus aroused is more likely to bring in people than would definite knowledge as to the nature of the address. General statements made or questions raised at the opening of a talk also arouse curiosity as to what the speaker is going to say. A person can make an audience inquisitive by opening an address on the subject of dealing with people by saying, for example: *How can we prevent the formation of chasms between man and man and close up those that exist? How can we plane down the roughness between employer and employee? How can we reduce those sandpaper irritations which cause marriages to founder, businesses to go astray, and international relations to grow tense?* In the course of his talk the speaker sometimes tries to impress a particular idea by making a curiosity-provoking statement before expressing it. *"There are three short and simple words, the hardest of all to pronounce in any language, but the man or nation that is unable to utter them cannot claim to have arrived at manhood. These words are—I was wrong."* Sometimes a public speaker exchanges remarks with persons in the front row, and thereby makes others sufficiently curious as to what he is saying to listen more carefully. A teacher intending to illustrate her talk by means of a drawing on the blackboard may pick up a piece of chalk considerably in advance, and thus get the students to listen to her preliminary statements. Teachers sometimes raise questions and dismiss them without answering them. They do so for the purpose of stimulating students to think on the subject involved. It is often a far better educational policy to stir up curiosity in regard to a question without deciding it than to decide a question without first stirring up curiosity regarding it. Some persons in ordinary conversation aim rather crudely to arouse curiosity through expressions such as, "I have something to tell you," and, "Shall I tell you what I heard today?" People buy grabbag articles not only for the chance of getting more value than they pay for; they do so also to find out what the wrapper enfolds. Many will eye through a knothole a thing that they would disregard if they had an open view of it. They tend also, despite their dislike for a secretive person, to listen to a whisper overheard and to read an advertisement that pictures an individual saying something to another in an undertone. Some secret organizations are formed primarily to attract attention, and through their secrecy attain their purpose. Many advertisers make indefinite statements about something to be featured or about an event to occur. *"Coming soon! Watch this space for further announcement."* An advertisement that provokes curiosity is called *teaser copy,* and such advertising is familiar to everyone. All fiction arouses more or less curiosity. The general outline of a work of fiction may be seen, and usually is, but not the details. Whenever fiction satisfies curiosity in regard to one thing it arouses curiosity in regard to something else, and each question that it raises may be enjoyed as much as its answer. A tale that is enjoyed, like a winding road, suggests something beyond the curve. Complicating a story so as to arouse curiosity as to what will happen next is a valuable technique for giving a fictional experience an effective hold on the reader's attention.

Curiosity is often aroused through sentence structure. This is done by building a sentence so that it comes to grammatical completeness only at its end. Anyone in reading the following illustrations finds that they arouse curiosity before they express complete thought.

"From as far West as Idaho,
  Down from the glacier peaks of the rockies—
From as far East as New York,
  Down from the turkey ridges of the Alleghenies
Down from Minnesota, twenty five hundred miles,
  The Mississippi River runs to the Gulf.
Carrying every drop of water that flows down two-thirds
    the continent,
Carrying every brook and rill, rivulet and creek,
Carrying all the rivers that run down two-thirds the continent,
The Mississippi runs to the Gulf of Mexico." [2]

"Sometimes gentle, sometimes capricious, and sometimes awful, never the same two minutes together; almost human in its passions, almost spiritual in its tenderness; almost divine in its infinity is the sea."

"If your brain refuses to follow your author, if your imagination is phlegmatic, if you will not take the trouble to stretch your mind until it can take in a vigorous conception, why, then, who can write a book for you that has any width, length or thickness to it?"

[2] Lorentz, Pare. "The River," Sequence 1. A United States Documentary Film. Used here by permission of the author.

A sentence in which the main thought is suspended is called a *periodic* sentence; one in which the main thought is expressed at the beginning is called a *loose* sentence. Most sentences are loose, and hence a periodic sentence may be effective not only because it arouses curiosity but also because it reverses the usual order and thus becomes striking. If, however, many such sentences are used they lose their novelty. A periodic sentence, moreover, puts a burden on attention in that it requires the entire thought to be kept in mind until the conclusion of the sentence, and so can easily be used excessively. But not to use a periodic sentence now and then is to overlook an effective means of awakening the hearer or reader.

After having aroused curiosity, whether in talk or writing, one must satisfy curiosity with something worthwhile, for people do not like to cudgel their brains for nothing. A person who baffles curiosity after arousing it makes the hearer or reader feel that he has not been repaid for giving his attention, or that he was tricked into doing so. As a result, the one who thus misleads another is disliked and soon forgotten. The person who presents a thing that has no more claim to attention than the power to stir curiosity usually does so with great peril to himself. The intense disappointment people feel over baffled curiosity not only indicates the need of fulfilling curiosity when once aroused; it also suggests the fact that curiosity is a strong force in our lives, and that appealing to it is an effective means of making life interesting.

CHAPTER IV

KEEPING UP SUSPENSE

SUSPENSE is a continuous state of ungratified curiosity, and so keeping up suspense is a matter of prolonging such a state. The methods of stimulating curiosity just discussed involve also maintaining suspense, for none of those methods satisfies curiosity the moment it is aroused. The problem of keeping up suspense, however, merits further consideration.

Suspense, being sustained curiosity, prolongs the change of experience that curiosity provides from the uninquisitive state that preceded curiosity. Its value from the standpoint of diversion is, therefore, greater than is that of momentary curiosity. In addition to diverting a person from his train of thought, suspense stimulates imagination, and so fills the mind with a variety of speculations. One is never more spontaneous and fruitful in thought than when in a state of suspense; never more free from monotony. For suspense to be most stimulating to the mind, uncertainty should be of a moderate degree. Complete uncertainty is too bewildering for speculation; complete certainty leaves no room for it. But a slight notion as to what may be expected is a cue to the imagination, and leaves it much range. The thoughts that arise during suspense are not necessarily pleasant; they may be forebodings of dread. Such thoughts divert the mind as effectively as do pleasant contemplations, but their disquieting effect overshadows their value as diversion. In upholding the use of suspense we have reference, therefore, to suspense that does not presage evil.

The joy of suspense is felt in recreation involving physical activity. Children enjoy the anticipations they experience when pursuing others or when being pursued in playing hide-and-seek; the hunter has many visions of game while tracking or lying in wait; and the fisherman repeatedly makes a good catch in his imagination while waiting for a strike. In all physical recreation the delay in the attainment of ends is enlivening.

People find much pleasure in planning and in preparing for something. The anticipation of any desired event fills the mind with many agreeable conjectures in regard to it. Young people contemplating marriage, and married people planning to have children make the future the present. Many make decisions in regard to their vacation much in advance and repeatedly muse upon their plans in great detail. As they wonder what their vacation will provide, their imagination supplies various experiences. The uncertainty of any pursuit creates suspense that provides visions of the future.

The mystery in anything creates suspense that stimulates certain persons to assume things beyond the veil. Wonder in regard to the origin of the earth and in regard to the creation of life has given rise, in the minds of simple folks, to many explanatory legends, and uncertainty as to what there may be after an earthly existence has provided them, as the following stanza from the negro spiritual "Swing Low, Sweet Chariot" reveals, realistic glimpses of a beyond.

> "I look over Jordan, what do I see?
> Comin' for to carry me home.
> A band of angels comin' after me,
> Comin' for to carry me home."

Many people enjoy mystery exceedingly; they like to be led through a labyrinth of design in which nothing is disclosed definitely. This is because while in suspense they have the enjoyment of pondering many stirring possibilities.

A state of suspense is experienced also when viewing many of the doings of other persons and many of the phenomena of nature. Any pending action or event that cannot be traced definitely beforehand may raise a question as to the course it will take and, consequently, lead to the contemplation of various possibilities. Even the pending action of a person with whom one is well acquainted may cause wonder as to what that action will be. Impending action often makes far more things go on in the mind of the person awaiting the event than actually take place later. Contests of all kinds may be enjoyed because the suspense involved stimulates the spectator to imagine various outcomes. The more evenly matched the contestants are, the more will be the conjecturing, and, consequently, the greater the pleasure of awaiting the end. A ball team that wins regularly may attract those who identify themselves with players and those who like to watch a well-trained team in action, but to bring out and to thrill large crowds there must be a "glorious uncertainty" as to the outcome. When the end of a game is a foregone conclusion, crowds grow weary and go home. But as long as "anything can happen" most spectators shiver in the cold or swelter in the sun to see the outcome of the contest. Sports writers build up an apparent equality between unequal contestants in order to hold the public in suspense for the purpose of creating demand for newspapers and for tickets to the athletic event.

Fiction and dramatic art make much use of suspense: sometimes suspense as to the outcome of a story or play, but more frequently suspense merely in respect to the incidents of a plot the end of which is discernible in a general way from the beginning. A reader of a story or a spectator at a theater may experience suspense either because of his own uncertainty regarding oncoming events, or because of the uncertainty experienced by a character with whom he identifies himself. It is possible to foresee happenings and yet be wrapped in suspense because of having identified oneself with a character made curious by uncertainty.

Thus, throughout the world of reality and the world of fiction, one can keep down monotony by keeping up suspense.

The maintaining of suspense is, furthermore, a means of keeping up interest in the presentation of thought. A speaker who in his opening remark says, "Later in my talk you will see why I say this," may thereby hold attention for a considerable period of time. There must, however, be a justification of such deferment, and expectancy must later be fulfilled if the procedure is to meet with favor. When a person makes a promise, and later fails to fulfill it, the hearer or reader feels that he has been tricked into giving his attention, and is resentful. Suspense aids in the presentation of thought also by making curiosity more intense. A deferment of its gratification often gives curiosity many times its original strength. Suspense, furthermore, serves to emphasize an idea, and thus to make a more lasting impression. In many works involving suspense, such as O'Reilly's "What Is Good?" both growth in curiosity and emphasis on the main idea intended to be conveyed are obvious.

> "What is the real good?
> I asked in musing mood.
> Order, said the law court;
> Knowledge, said the school;
> Truth, said the wise man;
> Pleasure, said the fool;
> Love, said the maiden;
> Beauty, said the page;
> Freedom, said the dreamer;
> Home, said the sage;
> Fame, said the soldier;
> Equity, the seer;
> Spake my heart sadly,
> 'The answer is not here!'
> Then within my bosom
> Softly this I heard:
> Each heart holds the secret—
> Kindness is the word!"

We see then that suspense renders the individual impressionable no less than it refreshes him by making him imaginative.

Although anticipation during the period of suspense may refresh the mind, it frequently affects actual experience unfavorably. Accurately to foresee something robs it of whatever novelty it might otherwise provide. It puts one in a position similar to that of a person who reads a novel after having been told the plot. As a rule, however, anticipation during suspense does not destroy the novelty of actual experience because what is anticipated generally does not closely resemble actuality. But, in a different way, anticipation often affects actual experience unfavorably. Frequently anticipation is governed by desire, and, in such cases, the real experience may disappoint because it falls short of what was expected or is different from it. Anticipation in regard to a journey to be taken usually involves no moments of enforced association with a boresome person and no privations or hardships, and the one who does not foresee such experiences finds actual travel that involves them disappointing. Persons who long visualize having a child of one sex or the other are disappointed more upon the birth of a child of the opposite sex than they otherwise would be.

"We planned to have a boy. We decided on a boy's name. We decided on his education, his career and how he would take care of us in our old age. . . . We talked at great length of 'he' and 'him.' . . . When they told me that we had a fine six-and-a-half-pound baby girl, I looked at my husband apologetically, and he looked at me apologetically, and we both looked away. We got used to the idea of having a girl, but I remember that for weeks, when people looked at me with puzzled eyes and wrinkled foreheads, I gulped and knew that I had called her 'him' again." [1]

Although anticipation governed by desire increases the disappointment of unfulfillment, rational anticipation of all possibilities does not do so to any great extent. It may lessen the novelty of an actual experience, but it is not

[1] Copeland, Helen. "Sour Grapes That Ripened." *Preludes*, Volume 2, Number 1, December 12, 1938. General Extension Division, University of Minnesota.

likely to lessen the novelty of all its details. Thus it is possible for anticipation to enrich the period of suspense with little unfavorable effect upon actual experience.

Let me repeat here what I said in my first book [2] in regard to the misuse of psychology. Because many people today are being grossly misled by self-seeking individuals who use psychology with sinister motives, we, as students of psychology, are interested in our subject from the standpoint of building up in ourselves and in others a protection against being exploited by designing persons. The surest defense against the unscrupulous use of psychology is to know how the self-seeker lays snares for the unwary. Such information enables a person to analyse the methods of others and thereby to detect selfish motives that may be couched in intriguing language. A common abuse of psychology is to enshroud things in mystery. As Dickens says,

"To surround everything, however monstrous or ridiculous, with an air of mystery, is to invest it with a secret charm and power of attraction which to the crowd is irresistible. False priests, false prophets, false doctors, false patriots, false prodigies of every kind, veiling their proceedings in mystery, have always addressed themselves at an immense advantage to the popular credulity, and have been, perhaps, more indebted to that resource in gaining and keeping for a time the upper hand of truth and common-sense, than to any half-dozen items in the whole catalogue of imposture. Curiosity is, and has been from the creation of the world, a master-passion. To awaken it, to gratify it by slight degrees, and yet leave something always in suspense, is to establish the surest hold that can be had, in wrong, on the unthinking portion of mankind."

[2] White, Wendell. *The Psychology of Dealing with People*, Introduction. New York, The Macmillan Company, 1936.

Every other principle of psychology can be put to wrong purposes as readily as that of maintaining suspense. However, I need not in this volume discuss further the misuse of psychology, since the building up of defense against exploitation is adequately served incidentally. The maintaining of suspense, although frequently put to wrong purposes, is a method of psychology in which everyone should be skilled, for by keeping up suspense worthy objectives can be served.

CHAPTER V

GIVING SURPRISE

Surprise gives change of thought suddenly, and thus makes change especially interesting. To any pleasant happening, unexpectedness adds color. Frequently one enjoys the suddenness of an experience far more than the experience itself. The suddenness of the most trivial thing can be amusing. "Our brightest blazes of gladness are commonly kindled by unexpected sparks." [1]

We like, of course, to have what is said or done conform to certain general principles, but unless our words or acts afford unlooked-for deviations within an accepted pattern of behavior they fall short of giving the greatest possible pleasure. If everything were completely foreshadowed, life would be flat and man would grow drowsy and irritable. In most human relationships there are no principles that are necessarily violated by an unexpected word or act, and, in such cases, one should occasionally endeavor to make life interesting by giving surprise.

That which comes unexpectedly not only gives pleasure; it also diverts the mind. Things that would otherwise escape notice are engrossing when they come swiftly. Unexpectedness often takes the mind from its moorings when nothing else could do so.

From the standpoint of education, unexpectedness has

[1] Johnson, Samuel. *The Idler*, No. 58.

value not only because of its possibilities for quickening attention and giving pleasure, but also because, by concentrating the mind on the unlooked-for thing, it furthers comprehension and memory. Any impression is more lasting when it comes by surprise.

In the ways of interesting people there is much unexpectedness that serves to impress an idea or simply to give pleasure.

1. Unexpectedness in Paradoxes

A paradox of one kind is a statement that seems contradictory before its true meaning unfolds. A remark that appears to contradict itself before its real meaning becomes apparent gives surprise because one does not expect people to say things that are in themselves contradictory, and such a remark gives another surprise later when it is found to have a different meaning.

"Man is never as truly himself as when he is acting a part."

"Our best defense against the United States," said a Canadian, "and theirs against us, is to have no defense at all."

"The trouble with us is not that we are ignorant, but that we know so much that isn't so."

In announcing the decision of the judges in a school contest, the speaker said, "Although there is only one winner in this contest, there are no losers."

"Some people will never learn anything for this reason: they understand everything too soon."

"New discoveries that are old."

"The injustice of justice."

"Beware of the fury of a patient man."

"The legendary age was a past that never was present."

"Seeing the invisible."

"The tragedy of growing old is the remaining young."
"That which is everybody's business is nobody's business."
"A good tale ill told is a bad one."
"The favorite has no friend."
"Beauty when unadorned, 'tis adorned the most."
"Some people never do anything because they do too many things."

A paradox of another kind is a statement which, although not contradictory, seems incorrect before its real meaning is grasped. Such a statement, like one that is contradictory, is startling because it is unexpected; the more unexpected it is when first heard and the more true it seems when grasped, the greater is the effect produced by such a paradox. Note the statements:

"If a play is by a good writer, it is a good play, and if it is by a bad writer, it is a bad play."
"The child is father to the man."
"There is nothing so fallacious as facts."

Similar to a paradox, is a statement that seems meaningless before it is understood. The saying of something that, before it is grasped, appears to have no meaning surprises at first because one does not expect anyone to say meaningless things; later, when it is found actually to have a meaning, it gives another surprise. Many statements of this type are intended to express finality.

"What I have written, I have written."
"Rules are rules."
"Facts are facts."
"If you have had your share, you've had your share."
"I am what I am!"

Almost any person, if he watches himself carefully, will find that he uses such expressions.

2. *Unexpectedness in Irony*

Irony is a sort of ridicule or sarcasm the intended meaning of which is the opposite of its literal meaning. A person may, to express disapprobation of someone, use words of praise in reference to him; to admonish another to remain calm, tell him to get excited. A familiar example of irony is the statement: The purpose of language is to conceal thought—not to reveal it. Irony very serious in character is that expressed in the last two lines of each of the stanzas of the following poem, which pictures in imagination the ghosts of fallen soldiers of various countries speaking in regard to their entering military service.

"I was a peasant of the Polish plain;
I left my plow because the message ran:
Russia, in danger, needed every man
To save her from the Teuton; and was slain.
I gave my life for freedom, this I know;
For those who bade me fight had told me so.

"I was a Tyrolese, a mountaineer;
I gladly left my mountain home to fight
Against the brutal, treacherous Muscovite;
And died in Poland on a Cossack spear.
I gave my life for freedom; this I know
For those who bade me fight had told me so.

"I worked in Lyons at my weaver's loom,
When suddenly the Prussian despot hurled
His felon blow at France and at the world;
Then I went forth to Belgium and my doom.
I gave my life for freedom; this I know
For those who bade me fight had told me so.

> "I owned a vineyard by the wooded Main,
> Until the Fatherland, begirt by foes
> Lusting her downfall, called me, and I rose
> Swift to the call and died in far Lorraine.
> I gave my life for freedom, this I know;
> For those who bade me fight had told me so.
>
> "I worked in a great shipyard by the Clyde;
> There came a sudden word of war declared,
> Of Belgium, peaceful, helpless, unprepared,
> Asking our aid; I joined the ranks, and died.
> I gave my life for freedom; this I know;
> For those who bade me fight had told me so." [2]

Irony, like a paradox, is effective because of the unexpectedness of the incorrect and of the correct meanings of what is said. The incorrect meaning may come unexpectedly because it is known to be decidedly untrue; the correct meaning, because it is perceived after the incorrect one was assumed to have been intended.

When expressing irony through speech, the tone of the voice and the countenance reveal readily the intended meaning. But when expressing irony through writing, it is more difficult to be understood. It is, however, possible to write ironically without being misunderstood, as the above examples reveal.

3. Unexpectedness in Stories and Plays

Stories and plays that were in every detail a complete fulfillment of expectation would be tedious, and so authors construct plots that involve some unexpectedness: unexpectedness as to ending, or unexpectedness in the development of a plot the outcome of which is discernible

[2] Written in 1914 by an unknown Englishman.

in a general way from the beginning. Unexpectedness of either type is illustrated by mystery stories. In early mystery stories involving crime the author had the villain prove to be the most unlikely person. But the reader soon caught on to this method, and so put his finger on the character that the plot left free of a motive for committing the crime, and free from suspicion. To take such a reader by surprise the plot was later constructed to involve the guilty one early in the story, and to clear him soon thereafter. In this way the average person was kept from suspecting the real criminal very long. Many other methods of misleading the reader so that the unfolding of the tale would give him surprise have been contrived in the writing of mystery stories. Because of numerous inventions and discoveries whereby life can be taken and the victim disposed of, writers of mystery stories today have at their command many means for keeping the reader from suspecting anyone in particular and of misleading him as to who committed the crime. A mystery story of crime may center on and give surprise in respect to any of the three questions, "Who," "How," and "Why," but those which center on and give surprise in respect to all of these questions provide the best entertainment.

To be accepted without protest, a surprising ending must on retrospect seem plausible and free from trickery. An unexpected conclusion that makes the individual feel that he might have foreseen the ending, or that he should have foreseen it, is especially good.

A surprising ending that is plausible may, when reached, give significance to facts or incidents that have been overlooked or thought unimportant, and so provide another surprise. It is the double surprise given in this way that underlies the enjoyment of many stories of the unexpected-ending type.

Many authors hold back one essential element of the plot until near the end and reveal it suddenly. In doing so, they give surprise that is not only plausible, but inevitable.

We all like a logical conclusion because we dislike to see those who tell or write stories distort the facts of life. But many people want a logical conclusion also because they enjoy being able to foresee the outcome of a story, and it is only in the case of stories that end logically that anyone can do so. The satisfaction of being able to tell how a story will end is the satisfaction of realizing that one has insight into the things portrayed. Such a realization often gives a very strong feeling of personal worth. People who get much satisfaction from being able to foretell events, and who take great pride in predicting accurately the end of a play are pleased more by *realized anticipation* than they are by surprise. They like stories and plays in which they can surmise events that the characters themselves do not in the least anticipate. They may enjoy a literary work primarily because it gives them a feeling of superiority for having greater foresight than have the characters. Many stories and plays of necessity portray a certain amount of stupidity, and so persons desirous of gaining feelings of ascendency find the theater a place where they can be freed from the blindness of everyday life, and have a sense of omniscience. With a vision of coming events, they watch the blind gropings of players, and smile at their stumblings, their futile quests, their groundless fears, or their unfounded exaltations.

To them, it is fun to watch the characters being fooled, but not to be fooled themselves. An unexpected ending would reduce such persons to the level of the characters from whom they had been holding themselves aloof. In order that they may have feelings of superiority and also the thrill of surprise, it is necessary to give them the ending that they expect, but in an unexpected way.

But people differ in their concern about being able to foresee the ending of a literary work. Some persons, aware of the intricacies and cross currents of life depicted in a story or play, and realizing that events cannot always be foretold, have no chagrin upon failing to foresee the last scene. They are interested in watching a plot work out, and not in being able to foresee the end. Other persons even refrain from conjecturing as to the sequence of events in order that they may enjoy the surprise of unanticipated happenings. Persons in either of these states of mind can enjoy greatly a logical ending that they did not anticipate.

Authors do not necessarily strive consciously to give either surprise or realized anticipation to the ending of their works. For the opening of many stories or plays there is an inevitable outcome, and the author's purpose may be simply to give evidence of that fact throughout the unfolding of the plot. Whether a person experiences surprise or realized anticipation in such cases depends on his penetration into the relevant facts of life. But authors who are more concerned about making a certain thing happen than they are about giving foreknowledge as to what is going to happen, nevertheless plan to give surprise as to how it is going to happen. Thus unexpectedness is an ingredient of all fiction.

4. Unexpectedness in Comparisons

Comparisons often reveal an unexpected similarity in things thought different, and are interesting for that reason. The statement, "The lunatic, the lover, and the poet are of imagination all compact,"[3] is interesting because it calls attention to a likeness in persons of different classifications. Figures of speech, like literal statements such as the one above by Shakespeare, are striking because they express a similarity in things thought wholly different. The statement, "Quick as greased lightning," suggests the extent to which one can point out, by means of figurative language, a similarity in things that are different. Children in growing up often learn of a similarity in things they had thought quite different. Because of arrogance or prejudice, many children are taught that the group of which they are members differs from other groups, nations or races. As a result, their later discoveries of similarities where they had thought only differences existed constitute significant experiences for them.

Just as some comparisons reveal unexpected similarities, other comparisons reveal unexpected differences, and are equally interesting. Persons who leave home expecting to find other people very similar to those of their birthplace are struck with surprise by every difference they observe. In studying primitive people, we compare their clothing, their tools, their conventions, their food, and their shelter with ours and are impressed either with the modernity of antiquity or with its difference from our age. A history book was given the title *Then and Now*,

[3] Shakespeare, William. *A Midsummer-Night's Dream.* Act V, Sc. 1, l. 7.

which implies a likeness or a difference between the periods compared. Many teachers point out a similarity in things generally thought to be largely different, or a difference in things generally thought to be very similar; and in doing so, they increase the effectiveness of their teaching.

5. Unexpectedness in Humor

Unexpectedness is a significant factor in humor. The suddenness with which an idea is presented frequently adds greatly to the amusing quality of what is said. A story-teller who carefully conceals his point until he is ready to make it, realizes that surprise is exhilarating. Since the nature of the illustrations to follow is now revealed, it must not be assumed that they will be more interesting than twice-told tales ever are. They should, however, illustrate satisfactorily suddenness in humor.

a. Making an Unexpected Statement:

"As a man was leaving his home one morning for his daily routine, he and his wife bade each other goodbye, and she added, 'Come again.'"

b. Giving an Unexpected Turn to One's Statement:

"At the opening of the new fiscal year, the treasurer of an organization remarked, 'Everyone in this organization is now one year in arrears,—except Mr. Smith. He is two years in arrears.'"

c. Interpreting Another's Statement in an Unexpected Way:

"Upon arriving at his office on a frightfully cold morning, a man got a telephone call from his wife, asking, 'Did you suffer on the way to the office this morning?' He replied, 'No, the breakfast was fine.'"

"In giving last-minute instructions to a servant, a woman planning a dinner for company, said, 'Now, Mabel, when you serve, be sure not to spill anything.' 'Don't you worry,' Mabel replied, 'I won't say a thing.'"

"A doctor once asked his patient, 'How much coffee do you drink, Elmer?' 'About twenty-four cups a day,' said the patient. The doctor exclaimed, 'Twenty-four cups!', and asked, 'Doesn't that keep you awake?' Elmer replied, 'It helps some.'"

"At the conclusion of his sermon a minister said, 'There are certain matters of business to be taken up, and so I'll ask for a meeting of the Board in the back of the church.' The members of the Board gathered as requested, and another parishioner stopped with them. The minister somewhat bewildered approached him, and said, 'There seems to be some mistake; I asked for a meeting of the Board.' The man thus accosted replied, 'Well, if there is anyone here that was more bored than I was, I'd like to know who he is!'"

d. Giving an Unexpected Turn to a Familiar Saying:

"A colored woman, much displeased with the conduct of one of her sons, said, 'Rastus am de only white sheep in de flock.'"

"Too many broths spoil the cook."

e. Foreshadowing One Thing and Saying Something Else:

"When I started out in business for myself I had only twenty dollars to my name. That was fourteen years ago. Today I am worth sixty cents."

"The difference between women and men is that women can be swayed by every sort of flattery; men, by one sort or another."

f. Calling Attention to Inconsistencies of People.
Consistency is usually expected of people, and hence inconsistency may provoke laughter. Comedians have, while

pretending to lecture seriously in favor of temperance, paused to take a drink of liquor, and, in doing so, have at least mildly amused some of the audience. Among the commonest inconsistencies of human beings is that of which Strickland Gillilan tells in "A Much-Bored Man."

> "How I dislike that man! Each time I say,
> 'Here is a view I took the other day
> When I was overseas,' what does he do
> But pull some picture from his pocket too,
> And start to show me something that can be
> Of not the slightest interest to me!
>
> "And scarcely can I start to tell him what
> My two-year genius said, but, like as not,
> When I'm not half way through—he will begin
> Relating, with a wide and fatuous grin,
> Some drool about the brightness of his brat—
> I'm bored whene'er I step across his mat."

In humor, what is said is as important as is saying it with unexpectedness. People like ideas that have a point or that express a truth. So, unless an unexpected remark has something for the mind in addition to unexpectedness, it does not arouse great interest. Unexpectedness is, however, never more important than when making a humorous remark.

Whether a person's purpose is to amuse or to instruct, unexpectedness in what he says often makes it interesting.

CHAPTER VI

VARYING THE VOICE AND PLAY OF THE FEATURES

THE voice and features afford many changes in manner of expression and need to be varied to hold attention and to make listening pleasant. Ideas that are new and garbed in fresh language may, despite their unusualness, go unheeded because of the deadening monotony of unchanging voice or gestures; while ideas that are old and expressed in commonplace language can yet be made attractive by the artist in speech. The person who lacks change in delivery may get much of the attention of those who have a vital interest in his subject, but he seldom gets all of their attention and seldom much of the attention of persons whom he must interest in what he says. A man who ticks like a clock is always more likely to put people asleep than to gain a hearing. Modulation of voice and varied play of the features are always involved in prolonged speech that serves its purpose well. There are several ways of introducing variety into one's presentation.

a. Varying the Pitch of the Voice. Pitch consists in the rate of vibration of vocal folds (vocal cords). It varies according to age and sex. The vibration rate of the vocal folds depends upon their length, thickness and tautness; long, thick and loosely drawn folds cause slow vibrations and low pitch, while short, tightly drawn and slender folds give rise to rapid vibrations and high pitch. For each individual there is a range over which the voice can readily fluctuate by means of rising and falling slides or steps in pitch. By discovering the pitch natural to one's voice and by letting the utterances fluctuate above and below that pitch level, pleasing vocal variety may be attained. To speak, on the other hand, on a constant pitch level makes one's voice as unpleasant as the repeated striking of the same piano key. The up and down play of the voice is as essential in speech as it is in music.

b. Varying the Quality of the Voice. The vibration of the vocal folds in producing pitch is a vibration of the folds as wholes. But the folds vibrate also in segments of their lengths, and the combined vibrations underlie the voice's quality. The quality of the voice is, however, determined also by the throat and other resonating chambers in the head. Some of these resonating chambers are subject to conscious modification and so make possible changes in the voice's quality. It is particularly in the expression of emotions that the resonators are modified, and, since every person is capable of making different emotional reactions, speech affords considerable variety in quality of voice.

c. Varying the Loudness of the Voice. Loudness depends upon the extent of the back and forth swing of the vocal folds, and the greater the amplitude the louder the sound. It depends also on the frequency of vibration because rapid vibrations deliver to the ear more energy per second than do slow ones, and because the ear is more sensitive to fairly high vibration rates than it is to low rates. Loudness depends, moreover, on the air chambers of the head and throat, which amplify the vibrations of the vocal folds. Loudness may be varied suddenly or gradually, and any change of force piques attention. Sameness of intensity, on the other hand, whether consisting of barely audible tones or of shouting, tends to put an audience to sleep. Unvaried loudness may, however, hold attention longer than unvaried force of moderate intensity because it is more unusual, but its novelty is fleeting. Those who must conserve their voices do especially well in observing the fact that it is not loudness, but variation of loudness that commands attention over a considerable period of time.

d. Varying the Rate of Speech. Rate in speech is the speed of utterance; the number of syllables spoken per minute. It depends upon the duration of utterance and upon the number of pauses and their durations. All good talk moves at an ever-changing rate; the time of uttering the syllables varies, and the pauses differ in length. Frequently the change in duration of utterance or of pause is pronounced. Any variation in the rate of talking, like variations in pitch, in quality and in loudness, tends to make people listen, and is a necessary attribute of pleasurable talk. A regular speech movement, on the other hand, is as wearisome as is a monotone.

e. Varying the Play of the Features. The physical features are involved in the expression of thought. And a gesture, whether consisting of a facial expression or of a gross bodily movement, when made repeatedly, loses its power over attention and becomes as wearisome as monotony in any of the attributes of the voice. The artful speaker affords not simply auditory but also visual variety.

The young and lively often strive for a novel effect by

expressing themselves in unusual tones and gestures. They may impersonate someone whose voice is familiar to their hearers, or speak in an unfamiliar accent. Those who give a dash of dialect are especially interesting. Some young people adopt the accent of a child learning to talk. A person who does so no more than once in two years and then only in conversation with a highly selected companion may, provided the tone he affects is not interpreted as characteristic of him, give tang to his speech. Impersonation is, however, a widely used mode of ridicule, and so is apt to be offensive to the one who is imitated or who is in sympathy with the persons mimicked. Unless engaged in with discretion, impersonation is, therefore, an ill-advised procedure. But when well executed, an occasional change of character assumed through impersonation is acceptable, and enjoyed because of the change of impression it gives.

To be able to vary the voice and play of the features readily it is necessary to be flexible emotionally, because the emotions control the manner of delivery more than does the mind. Pitch can be varied well only in the case of a person who has a pitch-level at about the middle of the range of his voice. But an emotional person has his voice keyed so high that there is no room for rising inflections, and they would be unpleasant if made. He, moreover, cannot easily lower the pitch of his voice because the emotion that he experiences tends to keep his voice up. Loudness, likewise, can be varied readily only by persons who have a general pattern of moderate loudness. But emotionality causes the individual to speak, depending on his general character, feebly or by shouting, and so makes fluctuations in loudness difficult. Similarly, the rate of expression can be properly accelerated or retarded only if the general speech movement is of a moderate rate. But expression in the case of many emotionally disturbed persons is extremely rapid; in the case of others, it drags. And it is as difficult for an emotional person to vary his rate of speaking as it is for him to vary his pitch and loudness. The quality of the voice, like its other attributes, can be varied readily only when the individual is not dominated by a particular emotion; when he is free to adjust emotionally to the thoughts that he expresses. Gestures are affected similarly; if the individual is dominated by stage-fright, anger or some other emotion, flexibility in the physical accompaniments of speech is difficult. An attempt to correct the voice of a person who has a tendency to persist in a particular emotional state without freeing him from that emotion is an attack upon a symptom, rather than upon its underlying causes.

The development of a varied delivery requires more than being unhampered emotionally; it requires also positive action. Much variation of voice and of gestures is attained through meaningful expression. The conveying of any shade of meaning involves some change of pitch, quality, loudness, rate, or gesture. Pitch variations are afforded continually by good speech. The expression of suspense, for instance, involves a rising inflection, as in, "What's that!" and the expression of certainty or of a promise involves a falling inflection, as when the bride says, "I do." Asking in a matter of fact way the question, "What has he done?" involves little change in pitch, but asking this question so that it implies that nothing was done involves raising or lowering the pitch considerably on the last word. Meaningful expression, furthermore, affords change in the quality of the voice because different emotions have distinctive tone colors. Seriousness, gaiety, sympathy, enthusiasm, indignation, and tenseness, when really felt, automatically produce different voice qualities. Meaningful expression involves also emphasis by means of variations in loudness. Note the change in loudness as you say, "It is not *work*, but *worry* that kills." In the expression of emotional attitudes, loudness is especially varied. Meaningful expression involves, moreover, change in the rate of speaking. Weighty or complex thought is uttered slowly, and important ideas are emphasized by means of pauses before or after expressing them. In the telling of events the voice usually moves at a fairly high cadence, and in the recounting of rapid events good talk moves at an unusually high rate. Saying what one means involves variations not only in all of the attributes of the voice, but also in the physical accompaniments of speech.

Although the voice and gestures may be varied much by striving to say precisely what one has in mind, they are not varied sufficiently in this way alone. The development of an adequately modulated delivery, no less than the achievement of any other objective, requires a conscious effort toward its attainment. It requires an appreciation of the importance of being varied in expression, and an awareness of one's shortcomings in respect to flexibility of speech. Most of us are as unconscious of the sound of our voices as we are of other sounds to which we have become habituated. In order to familiarize students with their speech deficiencies instructors now have them listen to phonographic recordings of their own voices. Most people do not recognize their voices when thus reproduced. This may be due partly to the fact that in speaking the individual hears his voice both internally and externally, while in listening to a phonographic reproduction of his voice he hears it only externally. But his inability to recognize his voice is presumably due more to having become unconscious of it. Everyone should listen to his voice or to a recording of it in order that he may become aware of his speech deficiencies and so be stimulated to overcome them.

To say that a person should listen to his voice does not mean that he should do so when appearing before an audience. Some speakers, especially amateurs, in listening to themselves, become self-conscious, artificial or mechanical in speech. They should listen to themselves only when preparing to give a talk. Others can observe their voices while speaking without suffering any of these evil effects. Such persons can advantageously give some attention to voice whenever they deliver an address. The most successful speakers give thought to their voices either while speaking or at other times, and strive to achieve modulation. So—

"Think variety. When you find yourself launched on a speech of some length, keep the need of variety on your heart. Even worry about it a little. Keep in your mind an undercurrent of determination *not to get into a rut:* be bound to use all you have; slides, steps, pauses, long sounds, short sounds, loud and quiet tones, varied qualities—all of that marvelous variety of which the human voice is capable."[1]

[1] Weaver, Andrew Thomas, Borchers, Gladys Louise, and Woolbert, Charles Henry. *The New Better Speech*, p. 226. New York, Harcourt, Brace and Company, 1937.

Varied expression alone, however adequate and appropriate the modulation of tones and gestures may be, does not constitute good expression. But it is equally true that no talk can be interesting; nay even tolerable, that is not varied.

CHAPTER VII

VARYING THE DOING OF THINGS OF EVERY KIND

VARIETY in the doing of things, like variety in verbal expression, attracts attention and often pleases. Much of the interest other persons take in what one does is due to the change of impression and thought that our acts afford. People like, of course, to have one's behavior conform to some general pattern. But unless a person varies what he does within an accepted pattern, he becomes brother to a machine. It is possible to attract and to please others through variety in the doing of things of every kind.

1. Things of a Personal Nature

In personal affairs novelty is often an attribute of things enjoyed. Clothes are frequently interesting because of their variety. A varied ensemble is preferred to articles of attire for the most part identical in material and color. And an occasional change of dress replenishes interest in the temporarily discontinued article. The enjoyment of having sport, street, formal and informal wear is partly an enjoyment of change of attire. A very effective means of attaining variety in dress is through originality. A dress designed in a new way may attract and please the eye of the spectator simply because he has not seen such a dress before.

In the selection of clothes people are not, however, guided chiefly by the desire for variety. The desire to be in style usually prevails over the desire for change. So strong is the tendency to follow the fashion that an individual will wear what is in vogue but unbecoming to him, rather than something else that would be more suitable. But fashion generally involves some novelty, and is followed for this reason, as well as for the satisfaction of being in style. Quality also may attract more than does variety. But there is a limit to which people forego variety for quality. Although interest in variety is not the primary factor in the selection of clothes, it operates significantly in the making of such selections.

In choosing clothes for the sake of variety, thought must be given also to establishing or maintaining individuality. Too many highly different clothes break up the personality into so many fragments that the one who appears in them has no identity. The wearing of clothes is a form of expression; and there must be congruity in what a person wears, as well as in what he says, if he is to be thought of as a distinct person. The one who appears from time to time in such highly different dress that he has no distinctiveness makes the big mistake of bringing out clothes instead of having clothes bring out his individuality.

The frequency of change of clothes is also a factor of importance. Infrequent change may give a pleasant surprise, but it may also make the wearer of a new garment uncomfortably conspicuous; very frequent change gives practically no change. Too frequent change also suggests over-emphasis on dress. Fashion has, however, decreed different dress for different occasions, and so by dressing for the occasion it is possible to have frequent change of dress without appearing to have change as an objective. By centering the notion of "well-dressed" in suitability, the individual is able to have a variety of clothes without appearing to have the acquiring of a large wardrobe as an objective.

Variety is involved also in dancing. Repetition of movement is an essential attribute of the dance, but unvaried repetition breeds monotony, and so the art of dancing involves repetition with modification. Variety is considered so essential to good dancing that the masters of the art prescribe the making of many improvised movements within the general pattern of the dance. "Modern dancing," says Margaret Wenner, "is less mechanical than formerly, and so permits much individuality in movement. It allows a man to lead his partner through a number of different foot-patterns with an ever-changing sequence. The more versatile and adroit the man, the more pleasurable may be his dancing." Dances also differ much; some differ to the extent of contrasting with each other. No dance program can be especially interesting without being well-varied.

In personal matters of almost every kind there is much desired repetition of behavior, but anything that a person does pleases another most when he varies the repetitions of what he does. Variety in the repetition of a personal act is, however, enjoyed not simply because of an interest in change, but also because of a realization that anything that is done differently from time to time is not done mechanically; that thought is devoted to it. Such a realization appeals to the pride of the one toward whom the act is directed. Acts of affection especially must be varied for the sake of paying respect to a person, as well as for the sake of affording him variety.

2. *Things of a Public Nature*

For gatherings to be of much interest to people they must provide variation of activity. Some persons in charge of gatherings rely wholly upon their own colorfulness to provide diversity, but doing so is usually inadequate and unnecessary. There are many other ways of putting variety into a meeting, and thereby making it more interesting to the members.

a. Having a Number of Members Take Part. The participation of a number of persons in the proceedings of a meeting affords variety because, as is said in an early writing, "Many Men, Many Minds," translated by Lawton, people differ, and the differences are remarkable.

> "Why, pray, did he who made us, as 'tis told,
> And all the beasts besides—Prometheus—give
> To other animals one nature each?
> For full of courage are the lions all,
> And every hare, again, is timorous.
> One fox is not of crafty spirit, one
> Straightforward; but if you shall bring together
> Three times ten thousand foxes, you will find
> One character is common to them all.
> But we—so many as our bodies are,
> No less diverse our natures you will find."

Because of the fact that people differ, it is possible for a teacher to enliven the hour by varying the classroom procedure in ways that cause expression on the part of different members of the class. The extent to which a teacher should do the talking depends on many considerations, but seldom should a teacher himself occupy the entire hour. Those who use the lecture method can greatly enliven the hour by pausing now and then for responses from some of the members of the class, or, if there are quotations or illustrations to be read, by having students read them. To overlook this means of varying the classroom procedure is to forego an effective means of keeping attention from wandering. Even lecturers who make an only appearance before a group can create a good effect by calling occasionally for a response from the room. Radio audiences are frequently given a program by two persons who converse or talk in turn. In amateur hours or political campaigns as many as eight or ten persons are put on the air successively in a thirty-minute program. To add further variety, persons of both sexes are brought on alternately. The motive in putting a number of persons on a radio program is often to convey the thought that many people share the idea of the broadcast. Frequently persons from different parts of the country are brought on for this purpose. But such programs also give much variety, even variety of accent, and so tend not only to suggest wide acceptance of the idea of the broadcast, but also to hold attention. In the church, likewise, much variety is afforded by bringing many people into activity. Scriptures are read, from time to time, by the minister, in concert, and responsively in a number of ways, by the minister and the congregation, by persons seated in different sections of the church, or by men and women. The saying of prayer is varied similarly, and there are moments of silent prayer, which afford a change.

In having members participate in the proceedings at

any gathering, it is important that the same persons do not always take part. If the same students are permitted to talk repeatedly, if the same brother is permitted to pray at every meeting and the same sister to testify, and if the same soloist, assuming that he is not especially talented, sings at every gathering, tedium develops. Secular and religious organizations occasionally bring in an outside speaker. In doing so they give much novelty to their program. Officers of all organizations are elected, as they should be, for short periods. If the same officials were carried over from year to year, assuming that they are not great favorites, many meetings would be more dreary than they now are. In deciding policies in regard to meetings of any kind, one should never overlook the enlivening effect of a new face and voice.

b. Providing a Varied Program. Usually the more varied the numbers of a program, the more enjoyable it is. Schools, in arranging declamatory contests, have both serious and humorous selections for their program, and they do not have all of a type presented in succession. Theaters provide amusements that differ from each other. Vaudevilles consist of a succession of separate performances, usually of songs, dances, acrobatic feats, short dramatic sketches, specialty acts, and sometimes also of exhibitions of trained animals. The numbers on such programs often contrast sharply. In designing amusement programs sameness should be avoided as much as possible, for, as Cecil DeMille said, "Variety is the mother of entertainment."

c. Rearranging Furniture. A very simple way of providing change consists in arranging anew, if possible, the furniture of a meeting place. Children and adults alike often find a rearrangement which makes the sections, the aisles and the direction of seating different from the former arrangement quite interesting.

d. Changing the Program from Time to Time. An occasional change of program is very stimulating. By providing a new activity or dispensing with a regular one, or by changing the order of procedure, a meeting can be made somewhat more interesting to the persons attending it. An occasional change of program, moreover, arouses curiosity on the part of the absent members as to what is going on, and so tends to maintain their interest. But an extreme variation in the proceedings of an organization might displease the members by making them feel that the organization has been changed in character. Even such a simple thing as change in arrangement of furniture might give a place an atmosphere of strangeness to some persons. An organization, like a human being, must maintain identity and yet afford variety; it must be always the same and always different.

Dullness of a meeting is familiar to everyone. When a meeting is drearisome it is usually so because its activity is of low quality, rather than because it lacks variety. But variety of some kind is always essential to the fullest enjoyment of any gathering.

3. Things of a Commercial Nature

Attempts are made widely to gain trade by doing things that afford change of stimulation. The format of publications is varied in unnumbered ways. Books, magazines, pamphlets, folders and cards are varied in size, shape, color, texture of paper, and in the design of the covers of books. Printing, other than that within the covers of most books, is also varied in size, color and style of type; and leaflets are sometimes folded in unusual ways. The make-up of printed matter is varied extensively because of a realization that to be different is to get attention. The format of good publications is, however, always planned in accordance with the principles of art because it is realized that, although attention may be had by means of a bizarre make-up, it is favorable attention that is needed.

Frequently the advertiser aims for a novel effect not through the use of words, but through the construction of miniature or colossal representations of his product. Such technique is effective in impressing the public with a trade name because anything uncommonly large or uncommonly small is very striking.

In the doing of these diverse things or anything else that is intended to attract or please other persons, change of procedure is as essential in one case as it is in another. Whatever is done, to sustain interest it must afford variety.

As was repeatedly stated, in striving to give variety to life it is necessary to avoid going to excess. A fact to be noted and always remembered is that verbal expression and the doing of things of every sort, to be well-varied must involve considerable sameness. But extreme sameness, like extreme variety, must be avoided because sameness of matter or sameness of manner makes a person a dripping spout. No matter what the aspect of expression—whether it be the thought conveyed, the language used, the tone of the voice, the play of the features; or whether it be something done or the manner of performance—to be interesting it must give variety.

PART TWO

PREVENTING UNWHOLESOME BEHAVIOR
DUE TO TEDIUM

CHAPTER VIII

CAUSES OF TEDIUM UNDERLYING UNWHOLESOME BEHAVIOR

MANY types of unwholesome behavior (wrongdoing and mental abnormality) spring from boredom, and are attempts to break monotony. The galling effect of an unvaried existence gives rise to more wrongdoing and mental abnormality than is generally realized. In this chapter I shall point out the causes of tedium underlying unwholesome behavior; in the next chapter, types of unwholesome behavior to which tedium gives rise. The analysis in this chapter of the causes of tedium underlying such behavior incidentally suggests means of prevention. All of the chapters in Part Three, which is devoted to the subject of furthering mental health, also suggest incidentally means of preventing unwholesome behavior. The causes of tedium underlying wrongdoing or mental abnormality are various.

1. *Monotonous Occupations*

In the work of many men and women there is much sameness which may ultimately become exceedingly tedious. Those engaged in unskilled labor, petty business, office routine, or household drudgery are often spiritless because of the monotony of their activity. The repetitive nature of work is increasing, and so the effect of monotony is of growing concern.

The individual's attitude toward repetitive work is influenced, favorably or unfavorably, by many factors in addition to sameness; hence it is difficult to determine the influence of sameness alone. Any of the following factors may make a repetitive task either more or less agreeable than its repetitive character alone would make it.

a. Satisfaction with the Pay Received. The worker who feels adequately compensated for what he does may be quite content with a monotonous job. Many young people earning money for the first time think themselves well paid, and, for this reason, may like their work regardless of the amount of routine it involves. Employees who consider themselves underpaid dislike routine work far more than its monotony alone would warrant.

b. The Extent to Which the Things Procured with the Earnings Are Enjoyed. The enjoyment that the individual gets from the things that he procures with his earnings colors greatly his attitude toward his work. No job is monotonous to youth if the money earned procures thrilling experiences.

c. The Basis of Payment. Labor organizations oppose the piece-rate basis of payment because they feel that it results in an increased rate of work, and in a decreased rate of payment as the rate of accomplishment goes up. But workers under the piece-rate system who are not alarmed in this way prefer that system to the time-payment plan. Many of them favor the piece-rate system at first because they think that they can earn more under it, but they favor that system also because it makes every effort seem more advantageous than does the time-payment plan. A girl wrapping and packing chocolates under this payment plan said, "It is pleasant to know that each box I finish means so much money at the end of the week." Her statement is typical of the answers given by the other girls who wrapped and packed chocolates in the same factory.[1] Whatever boredom these girls experienced in their work was, therefore, offset to a degree by the interest in it that the payment plan created.

d. The Ease with Which the Work Can Be Done. The amount of mental or physical exertion required by an occupation is always a factor determining interest in it. Many monotonous tasks involve decidedly less mental strain than do some occupations in which work is highly varied. In such cases, routine work may be preferred not because of, but despite, its monotony.

e. Opportunity for Advancement. To an ambitious person, a routine job is not unpleasant if it has a future; but if it is a blind-alley job, it is very drearisome. Much monotonous work leads nowhere, and may be disliked for this reason more than because it is unvaried in nature.

f. The Attractiveness of the Working Conditions. The working conditions, both material and social, have much influence over the worker's interest in his job. Most routine work may be pleasurable when these conditions are favorable; may be irksome when they are unfavorable.

g. The Individual's Health and Home Circumstances. The enjoyment of any kind of work requires a healthy body. A person in ill-health may protest against routine

[1] Wyatt, S., Fraser, J. A., and Stokes, F. G. L. *The Effects of Monotony in Work*, p. 34. Great Britain Industrial Fatigue Research Board, *Report Number 56*. His Majesty's Stationery Office, London, 1929.

work that he would not mind doing if he were in good physical condition. And home circumstances may color a person's attitude toward his occupation as much as do his working conditions.

h. *The Extent to Which the Individual Is Reconciled to Monotonous Work.* Whether a person is irked by a routine task depends much on the mental adjustment he has made to such work. Some persons reconcile themselves to routine. They may do so through the adoption of a philosophy of life, such as is expressed in the saying: "What cannot be cured must be endured." Many persons are also reconciled to routine by being accustomed to it. An individual's attitude regarding monotonous work does not, therefore, indicate how he by nature reacts to it.

i. *The Extent to Which the Task Keeps the Individual from Doing Things He Wishes to Do.* Boredom is often a misnomer for the irritation that an individual feels when a task keeps him from doing something else that he longs to do. Work interferes much with other interests, and the displeasure it causes in this way is often confused with boredom.

j. *The Nature of the Individual's Thoughts.* Many persons engaged in monotonous work keep up an interesting flow of thought by letting their minds wander. But many other routine workers dwell upon the unpleasant circumstances of their lives. They relive again and again past troubles, and cross the bridge to real or imaginary troubles of the future. Persons of a morbid nature find monotonous work disquieting, and grow irritable under its influence.

k. *The Dignity of the Work.* Our machine age makes little demand upon the intelligence of employees, and the

CAUSES OF TEDIUM

working and living conditions of many people are degrading. In the face of these facts, all our preachments about the dignity of labor fall on deaf ears. Many industrial workers today feel that they count for little in the scheme of things. No one whose self-respect is flickering can be happy. Workers who are distraught because of the degrading character of their tasks often grow morbid or wayward.

The influence of monotony and of these other factors in determining the individual's attitude toward his work is suggested by excerpts from answers that routine workers gave when questioned as to how they felt in regard to their tasks.[2]

a. "Sometimes I feel bored about the middle of the afternoon and would often like to move about or stand."

b. "It is sometimes a little monotonous about the middle of the afternoon, and I find it difficult to talk because of the noisy machinery. The machinery gets on my nerves."

c. "I like the work now but not when I first came."

d. "Sometimes the work gets very tedious, but I know that I have to work till 5 o'clock and settle down to do so."

e. "I like the work . . . The company is very congenial and we can talk when we like."

f. "It gets rather monotonous. The most interesting work is the assorted packing; sometimes it is a work of art getting them properly fitted and arranged."

g. "I prefer the straightforward work and dislike the assorted packing because there are too many different things to be done."

h. "I don't like the work and am bored almost all the

[2] Wyatt, S., Fraser, J. A., and Stokes, F. G. L. *The Effects of Monotony in Work*, pp. 44-47. *Industrial Fatigue Research Board, Report Number 56.* His Majesty's Stationery Office, London, 1929.

time. When I left school I did not expect I should have to work."

i. "In the afternoon I always look forward to going home as I play tennis in summer and dance almost every night in winter."

j. "The work is very tiring, especially to the eyes. I feel bored most of the time."

k. "I like the work fairly well but sometimes get bored. I begin to look forward to going home."

Thus routine work may be disliked by some persons for reasons in addition to its sameness; liked by others despite its sameness. This raises the question: Is sameness of work in itself ever a source of pleasure? Presumably never. It is correct to say that some persons like a certain kind of work even though it is monotonous, but there is no justification for saying that they like the monotony of it. Persons of high intelligence have a greater dislike for repetitive tasks than do persons of low intelligence. But does this mean that the intelligent persons dislike the monotony of repetitive work, or that they dislike other factors involved in it? No one today can answer this question. The indications are, however, that the monotony of a task is disliked by everyone, and that unless there are compensatory factors involved in a routine task, such as those mentioned above, the worker tends to grow sullen or wayward.

2. *Idleness*

An inactive mind and body make life drearisome; there is no lasting joy in indolence. Vacant hours create a desire for the passing of time. But the idle person lives each hour twice because time, with all its celerity, moves slowly for him who waits for it to go. It is difficult for those who are adequately engaged to realize how time goads the unemployed. The boredom of the unoccupied is a boredom that only the unoccupied and those who have studied them can understand.

Many persons who have nothing else with which to occupy themselves devote their minds to unpleasant thoughts of a personal nature. The torment that they experience in this way is often far greater than is the wearisomeness due to a lack of varied experiences. The unoccupied also experience much distress because of a feeling of being unimportant. Everyone likes to think that he is needed or that he in one way or another contributes toward the social good. Such a feeling is essential to the prevention of a warped personality. But those who are not engaged in any worthwhile pursuit may fall painfully low in self-esteem.

It is not only the totally unemployed who are wearied by idleness. Persons who are kept continuously at their work without being kept busy often find their unoccupied periods tedious. Almost anyone when in such a position, as most people are at some time or other, wishes that he were occupied steadily. A night watchman once complained about the monotony of his work, saying, "I'm a watchman, but most of the time there is nothing to watch." The indolent worker, likewise, is wearied by his idleness. Students or employees who lapse frequently into idleness suffer more from ennui than is generally realized. Employees who work under the piece-rate payment system tend to work more continuously than do employees who work under the time-payment system, and, in doing so, find work less boresome. This fact is presumably as significant in determining preference for a piece-rate payment system as are the facts previously mentioned. Thus idleness is a widespread factor underlying tedium.

3. Solitude

Much distress results from having a solitary life. Lack of human contacts may result in the frustration of various wants—frequently in the frustration of the want for variety because a casual sociability is for most persons a major source of impression and of expression. People are not all equally dependent upon social relationships for keeping down boredom, but many persons, when alone, go about quite vacant of thought, with their minds gasping for the stimulation of others. Some rural people, especially during seasons of mud and heavy snow, persons confined because of being physically disabled or mentally deficient, and especially prisoners who are required to refrain from talking with each other or who are prevented from doing so by confinement in private cells have inadequate human contacts. The history of many patients and the records of many prisoners suggest that prolonged solitude is a significant cause of morbidity.[3]

There are persons who have lonely lives even though they are not in isolated places or in confinement. Some have such feelings of inferiority that they seek isolation because they cannot be comfortable in the presence of anyone; others have such irritating attitudes that they have isolation forced upon them; and still others live quite isolated lives because they lack interest in persons

[3] Hobhouse, S., and Brockway, Q. F. *English Prisons Today*, p. 583. London, 1922. Also, Ives, George. *History of Penal Methods*, pp. 186-187. New York, 1914.

other than those of their own stripe. Anyone who does not care to know how people of another social or economic class, religion, nationality or race feel nor what they think isolates himself from one of the most fruitful sources of mental stimulation. Personal deficiencies such as these are responsible for more prolonged solitude than is isolation of home or confinement.

4. *Enforced Association*

It is, as I implied above, an indication of a well-developed personality to be interested in people of all kinds. But everyone, of course, prefers the company of some persons to that of others. And far more unpleasant than being unwillingly alone is being with someone in whom one does not take pleasure. A person may find the company of another unpleasant for any of a number of reasons; frequently because he is boring. The company of a monotonous person is especially irksome when it is continuous. There is often an acute in-law problem not because the in-law relationships involve unkindness, disagreements or an attempt to dominate, but because at least one of the in-laws is bored by being forced to live continuously with a person he did not and would not choose for a companion. Many persons have distraught minds because of being thrust into the company of unenjoyable persons, or because of having such persons thrust upon them.

5. *Lifelong Continuance in Monotonous Work or Living Conditions*

Some people grow weary not simply because of the monotony of their work or living conditions, but also because they must continue therein year after year. For many persons, twenty years' experience is, as Herbert Sorenson says in *Adult Abilities*, merely one year's experience repeated twenty times. It is not uncommon to hear someone who has long had a routine existence express desire for change. Much of the disillusionment and desperation accompanying middle life is the realization of being forced to remain always in the same monotonous niche in a world that abounds in diversity. The distress of women confined forever to routine in homes of narrow surroundings is suggested vividly by the following complaint.

> "There's al'ays th' same things . . .
> It's breakfast, an' dinner, and supper,
> Every day.
> An' the same dishes to wash.
> I hate them dishes.
> I smashed a plate yesterday
> 'Cause I couldn't bear to see it
> Settin' on th' sink waitin' for me.
> An' when I go up to make Father's bed
> I get seasick
> Thinkin' I'll have to see that old check spread again. . . .
> I hate lookin' out th' window,
> I'm so tired o' seein' th' path to th' barn. . . .
> I'm awful tired o' these hills,
> They crowd in so.
> Seems sometimes ef I could see th' ocean,
> Or a real big city,
> 'Twould help." [4]

Many persons are so extremely bored with their regular occupations that they give them up for work that is

[4] Lowell, Amy. From "The Day That Was That Day."

of an entirely different character. Some, bored not with their work but with the conditions of their lives, leave their communities and continue the same line of work in a new place. Much of the shortness of tenure of employees in all lines of work is due to a desire for totally different work or for change of scene. The desire for different work often accompanies, and is disguised by, a desire for promotion. Striving to get up in the world may, therefore, be motivated not only by a desire for a better position, but also by a desire for a different position. Some persons who have suffered prolonged boredom in every aspect of life make a radical break in their whole pattern of living. A housewife who experiences extreme ennui on every hand may divorce not simply her husband, but everyone and everything with which she is in any way connected in the community, and fly to a new place. The sullenness of some persons and the rebelliousness of others become comprehensible only when one takes into account the fact that they have had a monotonous existence for a long time.

Although there are persons who desire to sever one or all of their relationships and to establish new ones for the sake of change, many prefer their customary connections to wholly different ones. To live in the same place, to continue in the same work and to have the same associates simplifies life, while to make a marked change of any kind requires new adjustments, and so can become very disconcerting. The further man goes beyond middle age, the more he prefers his habitual connections, even though they may be quite monotonous, because they are less exacting. Habitual connections of an unvaried nature are, however, not necessarily monotonous; they may be very pleasing and preferable to new connections because of the things of the past that are associated with them. Many persons who left the familiar place have longed to return to it because life there was simpler and was enriched by pleasant memories. To live continuously in the same place also enables the individual to think of it as belonging to him, and as a place where his right to dwell is recognized. But all people do not find such attractions in their familiar connections, and those who remain long in a monotonous station which has no compensating factors are subject to developing extreme degrees of unwholesome behavior.

The causes of tedium mentioned in this chapter as factors underlying unwholesome behavior, although not the only causes, are the primary ones. We shall now consider the types of unwholesome behavior to which tedium gives rise.

CHAPTER IX

TYPES OF UNWHOLESOME BEHAVIOR DUE TO TEDIUM

ANY wrongdoing is an attempt to satisfy human wants. However extreme the transgression, it constitutes a means of gratifying desires that are not fulfilled in approved ways. Different transgressions are motivated by different wants, and any transgression may be an expression of a combination of wants. There are, however, many types of wrongdoing that are motivated primarily by the want for variety. In some cases the variety sought by the wayward individual is variety of emotional experience that the excitement of waywardness provides. What constitutes wrongdoing depends somewhat upon circumstances and point of view, but there are types of behavior that most people regard as usually constituting ill conduct and I shall treat them here as such. Behavior that is motivated by the want for variety and that is generally recognized as wrongdoing varies all the way from minor faults to crime.

a. Becoming a Truant or a Vagrant. The truant or vagrant may be wearied with narrow surroundings or lured by the novelty of going elsewhere. The child who strays away from school or vanishes from home, or the grown-up to whom every season is migratory season may be driven by boredom or may be acting out of curiosity in regard to unfamiliar places. There are many persons, old and young, who enjoy leaving behind the familiar and seeing what comes next in the road and where the road leads. Because of the drab life they lead, children in tenement or in slum districts are especially apt to wander the streets or highways for the thrill of making new observations and discoveries, and, in doing so, they often come to bad ends.

The passion for roving is not always motivated chiefly by the want for variety. Often it is due to a craving for a sense of importance. The child who leaves home may do so for the sake of adventure or for the purpose of making a parent, toward whom he for one reason or another feels revengeful, worry over him. The one who absents himself from school may do so as a protest against not being made the center of attention there, as a means of escaping ridicule for failure in his school work, or because associates dared him to "cut" school. To many youngsters it is a matter of pride to accept a dare. Truancy may also be due to failure to take school attendance seriously because of a disparaging attitude of parents toward the school, or because the child was frequently kept from school by parents for their personal convenience. Moreover, truancy or vagrancy may be due to a desire to escape punishment from a teacher or parent. Vagrancy on the part of an adult may be due to inability to maintain for long amiable relations in any one place, and because of a notion that the adjustments will be easier somewhere else. It may be due also to a desire to forget embarrassments. But in all cases in which roving is incited primarily by factors other than interest in change, novelty is, nevertheless, experienced and gives an impetus to roving.[1]

The impulse to be off and away is often blind; the individual does not know where he wishes to go or why, but only that he has an urge to be on the move. Some persons who are maladjusted to life have almost a mania for change of scene.

> "Change was his mistress, Chance his counselor.
> Love could not keep him. Duty forged no chain.
> The wide seas and the mountains called to him,
> And gray dawns saw his campfires in the rain."

Truancy and vagrancy frequently lead to various other wrongdoings. Many vagrant children, as a result of necessity or idle time, steal food from stores or market stalls, sneak into theaters or make acquaintances that often lead them into very serious forms of misbehavior. Furthermore, the vagrant of any age does not feel the restraints of settled life, and, as he goes from place to place, often escapes the consequences of offenses he commits, and so tends to repeat them. Truancy and vagrancy may, therefore, be far-reaching in causing wrongdoing.

b. Starting Fires for Excitement. Fires are exciting, and some children start them for this reason. To a child there are many thrills in a match, and his fingers often itch to strike one and apply it to any combustible material. Children having nothing with which to amuse themselves, and not knowing of the destructiveness and horror of a fire out of control, or unaware of how quickly a fire can become unmanageable, may attempt to break

---

[1] See Kline, Linus W. *The American Journal of Psychology*, Vol. X, No. 1, p. 61 (Oct. 1898).

monotony by starting a blaze. Many destructive fires have their origin in the fact that they provide thrills.

c. Engaging in Combat. Combat, whether physical or verbal, is often engaged in for the variety of emotional experiences it affords. Some of the emotions, such as fear or anger, aroused in an encounter are, in themselves, unpleasant. But they are, nevertheless, exciting and may be enjoyed for this reason. The one who picks a fight is often so steeped in monotony that he would rather be stirred at the cost of being harmed physically or socially than not to be stirred at all. Many persons upon whom tedium has settled heavily become disputatious and hostile because they like the excitement of combat. A husband and wife finding each other dull, and having no other absorbing interest, may, in their desperation, quarrel to fill the awful void. Even war is sometimes looked upon with favor because it breaks monotony.

"I passed some years in the most contemptible of all human stations, that of a soldier in time of peace. . . . I suppose every man is shocked when he hears how frequently soldiers are wishing for war. The wish is not always sincere; the greater part are content with sleep and lace, and counterfeit an ardour which they do not feel; but those who desire it most are neither prompted by malevolence nor patriotism; they neither pant for laurels, nor delight in blood; but long to be delivered from the tyranny of idleness . . . I never imagined myself to have more courage than other men, yet was often involuntarily wishing for war." [2]

Combat affords not only excitement, but also a feeling of importance for the victor, and the anticipation of triumph is usually the chief motivating factor of an en-

[2] Johnson, Samuel. *The Idler*, No. 21.

counter. But combat that is primarily motivated by the desire for a feeling of importance may also be motivated by the excitement it affords.

d. Inflicting Cruelty. The factors motivating most acts of cruelty are the same as those that motivate combat. Cruelty is, therefore, exciting in ways in which combat is exciting. The abusive person may be threatened with retaliation, and so may have some of the excitement that he would have if he himself were attacked. The one inflicting abuses enjoys the excitement of threatened retaliation especially if his victim is someone more frail than himself or an animal under control. This is because, in such cases, he can have the thrill of being pursued or attacked and, at the same time, feel secure. In some extreme cases cruelties are inflicted also for the novelty of witnessing agony. Animals of all types, and sometimes even human beings, are made to serve the thrill seeker in this way.

Sometimes cruelty, like combat, is due primarily to the desire to exercise power, and thus to obtain a feeling of personal worth. But even cruelties motivated chiefly by the desire for self-assertion afford also excitement, which constitutes an additional instigating factor.

Frequently persons are tortured in the guise of inflicting just punishment when the real motive is the desire for excitement or the desire to attain a feeling of importance. Thus lynching or tar-and-feathering is not done necessarily in the interest of establishing law and order.

e. Using Alcoholic Liquors Excessively. Although different opinions prevail as to what constitutes excessive use of liquor, everyone recognizes in thought, if not in act, that prudence demands some restraint in respect to drinking; that there is a degree of drinking that constitutes unwholesome behavior. What are the satisfactions that the bottle gives? The use of liquor often deals out to the drinker, for the time being, a happier world. Many persons when drinking heavily think themselves a success in every respect, and say or do freely anything they like. Such persons are also temporarily undisturbed by the monotony or other unpleasant circumstances of their customary lives. One of the most significant ways in which the use of liquor provides temporarily a fuller life is by increasing social relationships. Normally, the sociability of the individual is held in check by his prudence, his ideals, his feelings of inferiority, his taste for a particular type of person, his respect for another's interest in his company, or by convention. But under the influence of liquor self-restraint is removed and social barriers fall. Many persons irked by restraint drink and encourage others to do so in order to experience greater fellowship or intimacy, or to attain in some other way fuller lives.

Heavy drinking clears the mind of monotonous or other disagreeable experiences with the same readiness with which it removes barriers to social relationships or gives other satisfactions. A laborer in the Chicago stockyards, when asked why he got drunk so frequently, replied, "It's the quickest way out of packing town." The fact that liquor removes, for the time being, boredom or the thought of other distressing experiences is expressed facetiously in the statement:

"Do you feel that the endless monotony of your existence can no longer be borne—drink deep and you color your life to suit yourself. Do disappointment and despair gnaw at your love of life so that nothing seems worth while—some bottled 'essence of sunshine' will give new, fresh value to existence. Are you a victim of strange, uncaused fluctuations of mood so that periodically you descend to a bottomless pit of melancholy—well, then, why suffer, when over the bar a man will furnish you a release from agony? And so men of certain types of temperament, or with unhappy experiences, form the alcoholic habit because it gives them surcease from pain."[3]

The feeling of fullness of life and the freedom from care to which drinking gives rise has long been recognized, and has often been made the subject of discourse and song. These mental states and the mystery as to how drinking can create them have glorified by the creation of gods to drinking; such as Bacchus by the Romans, Dionysus by the Greeks, and Indra by the Hindus.

There are people who need to have some of their self-imposed or socially imposed shackles removed, but liquor removes them indiscriminately and often to excess, with the result that the individual himself or others are imperiled. People also need relief from thoughts of unpleasant things. But the individual who clears his mind of the disagreeable by means of alcohol usually has more to forget tomorrow, and so do they whose lives he touches. Many tragedies have resulted from man having unleashed himself and destroyed his judgment through the use of liquor. In the bottle, discontent seeks for comfort; cowardice, for courage; bashfulness, for confidence; sadness, for joy; and all may, because of impaired judgment, find ruin. Better ways of attaining a full and complacent life consist in the individual and society working together

[3] Myerson, Abraham. *The Foundations of Personality*, pp. 62-63. Boston, Little, Brown and Company, 1921.

toward personal development and toward the adjustment of conditions and of social attitudes in harmony with human needs.

f. Imposing upon Another Person's Time. An individual with a mind devoid of interesting thoughts tends to impose himself upon others for stimulation. There are many persons who, having no means of self-employment, visit too often and stay too long. They are as dependent upon others for entertainment as are children; they consume all of your leisure time and lean heavily upon your working hours. Inspecting a time-piece or speaking of urgent tasks are insufficient means of getting such persons to rise after they have once sat down. Like an autumn rain, they can be counted upon to last for hours. The more courtesy you show them, the more heavily they lean upon you for stimulation; call upon them, and they will repay your visit a hundred-fold. The one who comes because he has no other means of engaging himself is usually very unstimulating, and so he not only prevents you from doing other things, but also satiates you with his presence. The most unpleasant human relationships of many people are relationships of this kind.

> "Again I hear that creaking step!—
> He's rapping at the door!
> Too well I know that boding sound
> That ushers in a bore.
> I do not tremble when I meet
> The stoutest of my foes,
> But Heaven defend me from the friend
> Who comes—but never goes!" [4]

[4] Saxe, John. From "My Familiar."

This imposition upon your time becomes especially distressing when the mentally dependent person is a member of your household, because, in that case, it is even more difficult to be relieved occasionally from the demand he makes upon you.

g. Prying into the Personal Affairs of Others. Private matters that are not fully disclosed, like other incompletely comprehended things, may provoke much inquiry and investigation. There is presumably as much time spent in peering into another's personal concerns as in furthering knowledge. Curiosity is often lacking in social taste and in ethical judgment, and, therefore, is a poor master.

h. Betting. There are persons to whom oncoming events are of little concern. To them it doesn't matter much whether or not there will be a rain before morning, who will be elected, or which team will win the game. But by betting on the outcome of one of these things they become concerned in regard to it, and live in a heightened state of suspense throughout the intervening time. Those who bet usually anticipate winning, and their optimism gives favorable color to the stirred-up feeling of suspense. The anticipation of winning is, however, not a necessary motive for betting. Some persons are more concerned about making a wager than they are about their chances of winning. To them it is better to have bet and lost than never to have bet at all. Bets, entered into with or without anticipation of winning, serve to break monotony because they are exciting. Ennui has perhaps made more gamblers than has avarice.

When indulged in solely for the purpose of recreation, betting in itself does not necessarily constitute wrongdoing. A very small wager, although lost, may repay the individual adequately through the amusement it provides. It is, however, the weakest mind that requires this means of recreation—the mind that takes no interest in the issues involved or in the methods of execution. Betting small change for amusement, furthermore, leads readily to betting much money, and, consequently, to great evil.

i. Overstating Facts. Facts are often exaggerated for the purpose of saying something sensational, and thus getting attention. As the familiar saying goes: Report always makes crows blacker than they are; the wolf bigger than he is. Although untruths intended to amuse are often justified, an enlargement upon facts that govern the actions of people may in effect constitute the worst form of wrongdoing. Will Rogers once remarked to press correspondents, "The trouble with you boys is that you all want to write headlines instead of news."

These various types of wrongdoing suggest the extent to which frustration of the want for variety gives rise to misbehavior.

My discussion of unwholesome behavior has thus far been concerned only with wrongdoing. An equally serious form of unwholesome behavior often due much to boredom is that of mental abnormality. The trends of thought that constitute abnormality are many, and each has its own cause or combination of causes. Underlying most mental abnormality there is frustration of one or more of the fundamental human wants, just as there is such frustration underlying wrongdoing. Frustration of the want for variety is a significant cause of abnormality. There is an extreme lack of realization that boredom lies heavily upon the mind. In talking to a neighbor about his invalid wife who had become insane, a farmer said, "I can't see to this day what's driven her crazy. She ain't set foot out of this house for nigh twenty years." But it isn't only the layman that fails to appreciate that monotony plays a large part in bringing about abnormality. Some consultants of patients look only for frustrations of wants other than the want for variety. In writing of dejected people whom he had known as a physician, Hamilton said, "The internist is not apt to overlook unsatisfied cravings for clearly defined and highly valued satisfactions, but it has been my experience that country people and women everywhere and in all walks of life suffer a great deal from thwarted cravings for *adequate variety of stimulation,* and that this familiar cause of nervousness is too often not identified by physicans."[5]

Frequently an ailing person is assumed to need rest when, in reality, he is suffering not from overwork, but from boredom with routine. To such a person, rest is of benefit only because of the change of experience it provides. Men and women who are engrossed throughout the day in occupations are less likely to have nervous breakdowns than are those who have much time on their hands.

While there are many persons who develop mental abnormalities not because they do so much, but because they do so little, there are many others who have urgent need of rest; rest to gain strength or freedom from the worry that continuous pursuit of the occupation may involve. But the need of rest is less likely to be overlooked than is the need of change of experience.

[5] Hamilton, G. V. *An Introduction to Objective Psychopathology,* p. 288. St. Louis, C. V. Mosby Publishing Company, 1925.

Although frustration of the want for variety is a significant cause of mental abnormality, it is a *contributory cause of all types, rather than a primary cause of particular types of such behavior.* The boredom experienced by people is usually insufficient for it alone to derange the mind. But a mind distraught by the frustration of other fundamental wants disintegrates most quickly in a monotonous environment. This is because many types of abnormality consist in the individual's centering his mind upon himself. And a monotonous environment breeds introspection; it takes a varied environment to check it.

How can we prevent wrongdoing and mental abnormality of the types considered here? Prevention of such behavior is, as I stated previously, implied in methods for furthering mental health; methods to which the remainder of this book is devoted.

PART THREE

FURTHERING MENTAL HEALTH

CHAPTER X

PRELIMINARY STATEMENTS

THE interesting life is made up of a number of different activities and impressions, and each is varied somewhat upon repetition. Much of life's zest is due to diversity; much of its lack of spirit, to extreme sameness. The variety desired is, as I said in the Introduction, variety of stimulation, of thought and of activity, and often variety of any of these types of experience that involves change of emotional state. A few glances at human scenes will reveal that man enjoys going through different emotions. Many people find pleasure in attending an amusement park and entering an apparatus that jerks them in zigzag fashion, thrusts them into the air and brings them down with a thud, or which tumbles them over unexpectedly and sends them rolling. Such experiences are enjoyed because of the sensation of going through unusual and seemingly perilous bodily movements, and because of the thrill of escape from harm that they provide.

Many persons like to watch others subjecting themselves to hair-raising danger by walking a tight rope, entering a cage of lions, racing automobiles or by engaging in a fight. Dramatic and pictorial representations of such dangerous acts also give real pleasure to many persons. The enjoyment of seeing someone else exposed to great peril is usually similar to the enjoyment of actually undergoing seemingly dangerous experiences because people tend to identify themselves with others whose behavior they witness. Those who do not identify themselves with the dare-devil or the fighter, nevertheless experience much pleasurable excitement as onlookers.

Some persons, run to the scenes of tragedies and enjoy them even though they lament their occurrence. The lacerations of victims and the wreckage of an automobile collision, a flooded area or the ruins in the path of a tornado, although harrowing, may be enjoyed because they are exciting and because, like news of such occurrences, they give the individual the satisfaction of realizing that nothing of the kind has happened to him.

Although many persons enjoy exciting scenes, they enjoy them only for short periods. For the most part of their lives people prefer varied experiences of a tranquil nature.

Youth is more eager for variety, especially for variety that stirs the emotions, than is age. Most things to be interesting in the period of childhood must be somewhat exciting. There is the story of a young girl, who in reply to her mother's remonstrating against the risks that she was taking, said, "Mother, if it isn't a thrill, it's a bore!"

It is difficult to determine the extent to which the desire for novel things corresponds to age because it is difficult to find things equally novel to persons of different ages. To some mature persons of broad experiences there is little new under the sun. As a rule, however, interest in new experiences declines considerably through the years. But although the young and the old differ in interest in novel things, they differ less in interest in the mere novelty of anything. A child notices primarily the novelty of a thing, but an adult is concerned also about its other attributes. Age has learned that much of what glistens is glass, and so its reticence in reaching for something novel is not only a matter of growing old; it is also a matter of growing wise. The fact that age is more circumspect than is youth and makes choices on the basis of more factors in addition to novelty than does youth, can easily lead one to underestimate the interest of age in novelty itself. The interest of old people in novelty may be underestimated also because of having overlooked the fact that age draws more upon past experiences for change of thought than does youth. An old person, when apparently having little variety, may be watching scenes of the past rise before him in quick succession, and enjoying the dance of images of his earlier days. Although the interest of children and young people in variety is greater than is that of elderly persons, it is not as much greater as it might at first thought seem to be. Moreover, old people who are able to keep their minds occupied by looking back upon the trail over which they have come need, nevertheless, more mental stimulation than the past alone can give. No one can live by the past alone. In trying to further the mental health of anyone, we must always be mindful of man's need of a varied environment.

Although mental health requires, from time to time, something different, it is easy to be ensnared by the new. "Indeed, what is there that does not appear marvelous when it comes to our attention for the first time?"[1] En-

[1] Pliny The Elder. *Historia Naturalis*, Bk. vii, Sec. 6.

joyment due to the novelty of a thing is often thought to be due to the thing itself. And novelty is evanescent. It is a most perishable quality. Unless the new has some value in addition to novelty, it loses its attractiveness very quickly. Novelty without quality can be as deceptive as it can be momentarily delightful. A person under the influence of novelty is often completely out of his normal mind. He may fall in love with a thing that later gives him no flush of agreeable thought or feeling, but only cause for regretting his acceptance of it. Many persons are deceived by the newness of an otherwise worthless thing into exchanging an enduring value for it. They are left with nothing when the bubble bursts.

Some persons, aware that a thing attracts them only because of its novelty, nevertheless accept "anything for a change." Such persons may vote for a change of government simply because of their hatred of monotony or because of a desire to see what the new government would be like. Rebellions, although usually carried on primarily for other purposes, and sometimes for purposes that are worthy, may be fed much by a desire simply for a new or different government. The attitude of "anything for a change" is one of the thousands of examples of the irrationality of man, and generally leads to mental distress, rather than mental health.

Although the attitude "anything for a change" usually leads to folly, there are times when it is justified. For a person tired of what he has, an even exchange is often a gain.

"There is a certain relief in change, even though it be from bad to worse; as I have found in travelling in a stage-coach,

PRELIMINARY STATEMENTS 109

that it is often a comfort to shift one's position and be bruised in a new place." [2]

The continual gratification of the want for variety does not necessitate more and more elaborate experiences; there are other ways in which it may be served. This want can be gratified, in the first place, through simplicity. A woman who, over a period of time, provided a variety of food and table appointments for the members of her household or for her friends may give them an enjoyable change of experience in the simplest way by serving them a one-dish meal on the kitchen table. The wealthy sometimes find a "hard-time" party, which involves wearing very ordinary clothes and dining on simple fare, most enjoyable because of its novelty. The want for variety can be gratified, in the second place, through uniformity; uniformity amidst diversity, as when a person sees a large area of similar flowers or trees against a background of vegetation highly varied, or through uniformity between series of varied experiences. To a traveling salesman or a "globe-trotter" a week of settled life constitutes a novel experience. Uniformity not only provides change from varied experiences, but also makes the subsequent varied experiences more interesting.

"If all the year were playing holidays,
To sport would be as tedious as to work." [3]

Since the desire for variety can sometimes be fulfilled through simplicity, and through uniformity amidst diversity or between series of variations, it is folly to strive

[2] Irving, Washington. *Tales of a Traveller,* Preface.
[3] Shakespeare, William. *Henry IV,* Part I, Act 1, Sc. 2, l. 228.

always to serve this want by providing elaborate experiences.

Endless change is not only unnecessary for attaining variety; it is also unwise for other reasons. Change after change can become too exhaustive to be conducive to mental health. Frayed nerves frequently result from being perpetually stimulated by novel things. Another shortcoming of continuous change is that, although it makes every new thing fascinating, it makes nothing endearing. For a thing to mean the most to a person it must give him repeated pleasure, and so an article, a place, or a person to be loved must be experienced again and again. The longer an object has been owned, the more difficult it may be to part with it; the longer a church has been attended, the more it may become a place of worship; the longer a house has been lived in, the more it may become a home; and the longer people have been associated with each other, the harder it may be for them to part. The endearment that may arise from the repetition of an experience is not secondary to the interest that novelty creates. But repetitions of anything should, within certain limits, be varied so as to afford some novelty.

The variety that an individual may enjoy depends upon himself and upon his surroundings. The richer he is in ideas and in capabilities, the less he is restricted by the circumstances of his life in having broad experiences. "I do pity," said Falkland, "an unlearned gentleman on a rainy day." The internal resources of most people are, as a matter of fact, very limited; they can have ideas and excitement from their own store of previous activities and impressions for only a short time. Then there ensues an intense yearning for somebody or something that will take up their attention and give direction to their thoughts and actions. Personal development is by far the best safeguard against monotony. But the attainment of the full life is not solely an individual matter; it is, to a considerable extent, a matter of circumstances beyond the individual's control. It is for us, therefore, to consider the furtherance of mental health through both individual and community enterprise.

CHAPTER XI

ENABLING EVERYONE TO HAVE SOMETHING TO DO

Man, being by nature active, likes to be mentally and physically engaged. Watch the faces of those who do one thing or another and you often see that merely being active creates interest in life. Watch also the faces of those who have nothing to do and you see that they express no animation. That a person likes to be mentally and physically engaged is implied when he says, in reference to an otherwise futile act of his, "It gives me something to do." The attainment of the greatest happiness necessitates a fully occupied mind. A familiar statement of this thought is, "A mind quite vacant is a mind distress'd." [1] Much of the enjoyment of being fully occupied is due to the variety and to the diversion from unpleasant circumstances it provides.

The need of being occupied may be served by work or other activity. Work serves this need especially well because it provides constant employment of both mind and body during working hours, and, at other times, to the mind by prompting it to plan for the morrow. Much of the enjoyment that people get from their work is in having something to get up for in the morning, something to plan for, something to go to.

[1] Cowper, William. "Retirement," l. 623.

The necessity of making a livelihood drives most people to employing their minds or bodies, and, for this reason, we may agree that necessity is often a blessing in disguise. Some of the leisure class, because of economic security, frequently fail to satisfy their need for something to think of and to do. They lie in bed in the morning because there is nothing to get up for; they take their morning walk if not too tired; they sit down and persuade themselves that they sit down to think, but find it impossible to think much without an urgent subject. Many who are at liberty to do as they choose confess that they are unhappy because they do not have regular employment. The following explanation made two hundred years ago of tedium drifted into upon gaining economic security is equally explanatory of the tedium of some of the leisure class of today.

"Being enabled, by the death of an uncle, to live without my pay, I quitted the army, and resolved to regulate my own motions. I was pleased for a while, with the novelty of independence, and imagined that I had now found what every man desires. My time was in my own power, and my habitation was wherever my choice should fix it. I amused myself for two years in passing from place to place, and comparing one convenience with another; but being at last ashamed of inquiry, and weary of uncertainty, I purchased a house and established my family.

"I now expected to begin to be happy, and was happy for a short time with that expectation. But I soon perceived my spirits to subside, and my imagination to grow dark. The gloom thickened every day around me, I wondered by what malignant power my peace was blasted, till I discovered at last that I had nothing to do."[2]

[2] Johnson, Samuel. *The Idler*, No. 21.

Although freedom from the necessity of making a livelihood often results, as in the case of the ex-soldier, in idleness, it does not necessarily do so. Many persons who have economic security nevertheless take up work and find it engrossing. It is pursuing work (not pursuing it out of necessity) that gives employment to the mind and body.

Work may be enjoyed not only because it is engrossing, but also because it enables the individual to feel that he counts for something. And such satisfaction is as important to him as is employment of his mind and body. The self-regard experienced by the worker is especially great if what he does is of social benefit. The value of work of this character to the individual, and to society as well, makes it the most satisfactory type of activity. In a well-ordered society a useful occupation would always be available to every able person.

Those who, for one reason or another, are unable to take up work in the ordinary sense of the word need other activity. Persons in hospitals for the mentally or physically disabled benefit greatly from occupational or recreational therapy. Such activity may serve significantly, although usually to a less degree, the three ends of work mentioned above; it may engross the mind interestingly, divert it from unpleasant thoughts, and afford the individual a sense of importance either because of the usefulness of what he does or simply because it requires skill. A man who was confined to a mental hospital is on record as having recovered from a rather serious disorder through his ability to defeat all comers at Ping Pong.

The value of therapeutic activity in hospitals depends upon its nature and its suitability for the patient. Novel activity is more engaging than familiar routine, and so has greater value as treatment for many individuals. Those who have a tendency to sink into depression or to engage excessively in daydreaming have special need for unusual employment, and the more alien the line of activity is to such a person's previous experience, the better it serves its purpose of engaging his mind. But for patients who are in extreme states of excitement, repetitive operations are soothing, and, therefore, preferable to highly varied activity. Institutional work that is occupational in character, such as the making and repairing of things to be used or sold by the hospital and the doing of things involved in the operation of the hospital, may be enjoyed by some patients because it gives them a feeling of being useful, but other patients may look upon such operations as drudgery and find them depressing. Work that prepares the patient for a career to be followed upon his release from the hospital may make him hopeful, but unless he has an interest in it, such training has little therapeutic value.

Persons in institutions for the feeble-minded also need occupational and recreational therapy. In recent years many institutions for such persons have been turned from places of considerable apathy into places of much activity involving simple study, different work projects and a variety of play activities. Where this has been done there is a surprising amount of contentment and happiness.

Prisoners, like the mentally and the physically sick and the feeble-minded, need activity; but, unlike such persons in general, most prisoners have very little to do. They are restricted in the production of articles of commerce by legislation designed to protect private enterprise that would be affected by the competition of prison-manufactured articles,[3] and are denied such therapeutic work as is afforded in hospitals. Reasonable employment during the term of incarceration would somewhat preserve the individual's mind, and thus provide a safeguard against unwholesome behavior subsequent to release from prison.

Persons forced out of their work by their age are, likewise, in need of something to do to engross the mind and to maintain self-esteem. The amount of activity needed depends somewhat upon the amount to which one is accustomed, and so those who are very active in their occupations have, upon retirement, great need of other employment. Unless retired persons, especially those who were highly active in their work, find something else to do they wither quickly. With a lowering of the age at which men and women are retired from their work, the providing of activity for those who have served their time in their vocations is becoming increasingly important. A retirement plan should consist not only of a plan for subsistence; it should consist also of a plan for light work or other activity.

Although work as a means of engrossing the mind is the most satisfactory type of pursuit, everyone requires, of course, also a variety of other activities. In this chapter in which I emphasized the need of either work or other activity, rather than the need of both, I presented merely the minimum requirement of mental health. Later chapters are devoted to the need of broad experiences.

[3] See Bennett, James V. "Horse Collars and Prisons." *Survey*, Mid-monthly Issue, Vol. LXXIII, No. 9, pp. 277-279 (September, 1937).

CHAPTER XII

AFFORDING OCCASIONAL CHANGE OF WORK

THOSE who have work are spared the monotony of idleness; but if their tasks are of a very routine sort, they may find them almost as wearisome as unemployment. And the wearisomeness of routine not only distresses the worker; it also hinders accomplishment. Practical requirements of industry make monotonous work inevitable. But boredom with repetitive work can be lessened through occasional change of such work. Except insofar as employees have a preference for certain tasks, they prefer doing various types of routine work throughout the day to doing a single type continuously.

What are the comparative effects of variety and of uniformity in work upon accomplishment? An investigation has been made of the comparative effects of variety and of uniformity of operation in several kinds of work.[1] One type of work to which this investigation was devoted consisted of handkerchief folding. On some days the handkerchiefs were folded in two styles, the oblong and the French style, and the style of folding was changed every hour. On other days, the folding was done in only one style throughout the day. Although the movements

[1] Wyatt, S., and Fraser, J. A. *The Comparative Effects of Variety and Uniformity in Work.* Industrial Fatigue Research Board, Report Number 52. London, His Majesty's Stationery Office, 1928.

in the two styles of folding were fairly similar, the styles differed considerably in appearance. Eight girls were observed for a period of three weeks, and the average hourly accomplishment for this period in terms of dozens was determined. As will be noted below, accomplishment was slightly greater in the varied work program.

Average Hourly Accomplishment on Days of Uniform Folding and on Days of Varied Folding

Girl	A	B	C	D	E	F	G	H
Uniform folding	27.8	27.5	24.1	26.3	24.9	27.1	22.8	24.6
Varied folding	27.9	28.0	24.8	26.4	24.5	26.9	23.7	24.9
Per cent difference [2]	.4	1.8	2.9	.4	—1.6	—.7	3.9	1.2

Another type of work to which this investigation was devoted is that of soap wrapping. On the days of varied work, the girls first went to the storeroom for 144 cakes of soap and for the same number of wrappers. Then 72 of these cakes were wrapped in wax paper and in an outer wrapper, the ends of the wrappers gummed and labeled, and the wrapped cakes packed three in a box. The girls then changed from a sitting to a standing position and wrapped the filled boxes into packages of four boxes, sealed and labeled the ends, and placed the packages in a wooden case. The remaining 72 cakes of soap were then treated in the same manner, and the wooden cases carried to a conveyer at some distance away. On

[2] Per cent difference in accomplishment is computed on the basis of accomplishment in uniform folding.

other days, the girls were placed at a bench to which soap was supplied by a conveyer, and the girls only wrapped the soap and packed it into boxes of three. This experiment involved six girls who worked five days at the varied tasks and five days at the uniform task. The results, given below, indicate that accomplishment was greater on days of unvaried work. But the difference in accomplishment in the varied and unvaried work is not great. The results of this part of the study are, therefore, not significant.

Average Number of Cakes Wrapped and Packed Per Hour for Uniform Work and for Varied Work

Girls	A	B	C	D	E	F
Uniform work	194.2	246.0	243.8	223.6	245.5	214.3
Varied work	185.7	240.9	237.3	222.5	230.2	206.9
Per cent difference	—4.4	—2.1	—2.7	—.5	—6.2	—3.5

Other types of work to which this investigation was devoted are bicycle chain assembly, cartridge case assembly, tobacco weighing and cigarette making. The results of these studies favored varied work. In regard to the results of these and the two studies reviewed above combined it may be said that

    a. Varied forms of work are generally more productive than is uniformity in method of procedure.

    b. The highest output is obtained when the form of activity is changed after one and one-half or two hours of unvaried work.

c. Many changes are detrimental to output because of their interference with the swing of work.

This investigation of the comparative effects of variety and uniformity in work is limited to a few types of work —only six types of work were involved—and the number of workers studied in each case was small. For these reasons the conclusions of this study must be regarded as having a limited application. But this study is very reliable, and, therefore, valuable insofar as it goes. To know of the comparative effects of variety and of uniformity of operation in other types of work, further investigation is necessary.

The need of change of work on the part of the individual depends somewhat on the number and proximity of other workers and on the amount of communication he has with them. Most isolated individuals are more susceptible to boredom than those working within reach of others because social stimulation often constitutes a good antidote to boredom.

The frequency with which change of work should be afforded depends also on the monotony of the work done. A task that is completely automatic is less tedious than one only partly automatic. This is because anything that can be done automatically requires little attention, and so leaves the mind free for other things. An individual whose mind has been disengaged from the task may obtain pleasing variety by exchanging grimaces or remarks with other workers, by planning a social event or a vacation, by giving thought to an intellectual subject, or by simply letting the mind wander. Individuals engaged in highly routine work have indicated by their remarks that they obtain many such satisfactions while at work.³

"Often my thoughts wandered and were concerned with my forthcoming holidays."

"My thoughts wandered extensively . . . , but strange to say I believe I worked much better during those periods."

"The occasions when my thoughts wandered were most pleasant and helped to prevent monotony."

"Interesting thoughts and pleasant reminiscences certainly help to prevent monotony in my case."

"When thoughts are on other matters or problems, monotony is absent."

"Occasionally I found myself theorizing and not attending to the work in hand, and continued to do so until some distraction occurred. Time seemed to pass quickly and pleasantly on these occasions."

All of us when engaged in routine work have occasionally given rein to fancy.

> "Then danced we on the wrinkled sand
> Sat in cool caverns by the sea,
> Or wandered up the bloomy land,
> To talk with shepherds on the lea." ⁴

Completely automatic work not only leaves the mind freer to wander than does work that is partly automatic, but is also less vexing. When performing a semi-automatic task the mind finds many opportunities to roam, but as it wanders it is presently called back to the task.

³ Wyatt, S., Fraser, J. A., and Stokes, F. G. L. *The Effects of Monotony in Work.* Industrial Fatigue Research Board, Report Number 56, p. 36. London, His Majesty's Stationery Office, 1929.
⁴ Bryant, William C. From "A Day-Dream."

Work that permits the mind to wander but always jerks it back is more agitating than is work that demands continuous attention. A person whose work is semi-automatic may, therefore, have as much or greater need of change of work than the person whose work is completely automatic.

Although completely automatic work is pleasant to some because it frees their minds for other things, it is equally unpleasant to others for the same reason. To find pleasure through mind-wandering it is necessary to have had significant experiences. Employees who have never had anything but a narrow life find few sparkling thoughts in the recesses of their minds. Likewise, those who are of a morbid nature are usually happier in tasks that occupy their minds completely than they are in tasks that permit their minds to wander. The mind must have engagements, and the engagements must be pleasant for automatic work to be enjoyed. A vacant or agitated mind may find completely automatic work most unpleasant. Such persons have the greatest need of change of work if what they do is of a highly routine sort.

Since many persons enjoy routine work because it enables their minds to wander, their need for change of work can be decreased by making their work automatic. Monotonous work can be made automatic by establishing and adhering to a routine in carrying on such work. Many persons in domestic life and in industry make monotonous work automatic by deciding upon a place for everything and by putting everything in its place, by having regular times for doing things, and by performing the parts of a task in regular sequence. The housewife who, to the contrary, must look for everything she uses, and later for a place to put it; workers in general who, because of performing their tasks in irregular order, must use all their wits occasionally to determine whether they have done everything that should be done, keep their minds continually at things that might well be left to the hand. Reducing work to routine not only permits the mind to wander; it also results in the doing of work in less time. And, for many people, work done in less time results in greater leisure. By routinizing work it is often possible to set the mind free to such a remarkable extent that change of work is not greatly needed or desired.

Many investigations have been made in the field of education to determine the proper length of lesson periods for children of different ages. These, together with observation of children at school, reveal that young children are incapable of giving prolonged attention to any subject, and have resulted in frequent change of study for them. It is recognized that in the case of high school and college students certain studies, such as mathematics, should not be continued for more than an hour; crafts, such as drawing and needlework may be continued much longer. Throughout the educational system some change of subject seems necessary to break monotony and to maintain interest. But change of subject before a thread of thought has been well formed or before a pattern of thought has been completed may result in wasted effort. In education, as in industry, change of work can be too frequent, as well as not frequent enough. It is vexing to some learners to be forced to lay aside a subject before they are ready to do so, as it is vexing to others to be kept constantly on one subject. And accomplishment may be hindered as severely by too frequent change as by too continuous application to one subject. The frequency with which a new subject should be taken up depends on the subjects studied and on the student himself. The only general rule that can be laid down is that one should be mindful of the need of change and mindful of the need of connected study, and that one should vary the work with discretion.

CHAPTER XIII

AFFORDING DUE LEISURE FOR ALL

LEISURE is time in excess of that required for making a living, and is essential to the welfare of man. Its value is two-fold. Leisure makes possible, in the first place, recovery from boredom and other evil effects of work. The tedium of most work is today much greater than formerly. The colonists found their occupations varied and exciting; they roamed nature's diversified tracts in pursuit of wild game, they worked together in building homes and in gathering fuel, and they joined hands in protecting themselves against attack. The repetitive character of tasks and the lack of communication between workers in modern industry contrast sharply with the varied nature of work in the early American days, and the tendency toward routinism is increasing in most occupations. This trend makes more and more urgent the providing of leisure as a means of mitigating the wearisomeness of unvaried work. Leisure also gives rest to a fatigued body and often diverts a disquieted mind from whatever unpleasantness there may be about the work. Thus, leisure frees the individual, for the time being, from any of the evil effects of work.

Leisure makes possible, in the second place, the doing of various interesting things. The happy life is a life that affords considerable leisure to do what one wishes to do, and the humanitarian attitude concedes to the individual a right to such a life. The amount of leisure depends on the extent to which the occupation provides the satisfactions essential to complete living; the fewer the satisfactions which work provides, the greater the need of leisure for doing things apart from work. The occupations of many people today provide merely subsistence, and the need of subsistence is not half of the needs of life. Persons constantly leashed to the job, especially those whose work is of a very uninteresting kind, find very limited opportunity for the pursuit of happiness. To provide people with leisure in order that they may live more fully is one of the highest social objectives. As a people, we must be not only "work-minded"; we must be also "leisure-minded."

The doing of things for the pleasure they afford has not always been looked upon with favor. The pioneers' hard struggle in the wilderness left them little time for diversion, and so they developed a philosophy that extolled work and opposed recreation. They did countenance some leisure, but only to the extent which made possible the resuming of work more effectively. Energy devoted to recreation that was fatiguing, and hence rendered the individual less able to work, was called misspent. Puritanism denounced the pursuit of the pleasures of life as worldliness, and so it too was a factor in the establishment of the belief that not recreation, but only toil, was honorable. The change of view regarding the respectability of engaging in pleasurable activity is due, on the one hand, to the simplification of the problem of production, which now makes long hours of toil unnecessary. With the decrease in the need for labor, a more tolerant attitude regarding the doing of other things for enjoyment was inevitable. The acceptance of the view that time should be provided for recreation is due, on the other hand, to a growing realization that a diversified life is essential to mental health; that no one can be happy who is forever in a groove.

Society now has much free time on its hands. It is equally true, however, that there are many people who are poorly housed, poorly fed, poorly clothed and who have inadequate medical care. Much of our spare time as a people should be devoted to procuring the things that physical well-being requires. But apart from the time needed to procure such necessities, society has much leisure time that may be devoted to serving the individual's mental and emotional needs, and more leisure due to greater economies in production seems to be in the offing. We as a people, therefore, are not confronted with the problem of obtaining more leisure. The free time that we have is, however, not apportioned properly. Our problem is to distribute it more equitably.

There is also the problem of deciding how an individual's free time should be apportioned; whether it should consist of much leisure at long intervals, or of some other allotment. To serve both of its purposes there should be different apportionments of leisure. From the standpoint of breaking monotony, frequent and short periods of free time are more suitable than long and infrequent ones; for enabling the individual to do things he wishes to do, longer periods than are necessary for breaking monotony are required. In order that both of the needs for leisure may be served there must, therefore, be various allotments of free time.

1. Daily Intermissions

"The work, divided aptly, shorter grows."

A brief respite in routine several times a day may keep down tedium by relieving the worker before he becomes really bored. Teachers give children recess periods because they have long known that all work and no play makes Jack a dull boy. The housewife who puts her work aside occasionally for a walk to the corner store or for a short drive; the business or professional man who saunters, now and then, around the block or merely watches the stream of commerce from his window; and the office or factory worker who is given a brief intermission, all find that the breaking of the day averts boredom. The value of recess periods has been a subject of much investigation in industry, and such studies indicate that short intermissions have a favorable effect both on accomplishment and on the feelings of well-being.[1] It is apparent that intermission serves mainly one of the objectives of leisure; that of refreshing the individual so that he will find it easier to continue working. They are too brief to enable the doing of anything of particular interest, and so other apportionment of leisure is also necessary.

2. Short Work Days

A decrease in working hours may, like daily intermissions, avert tedium by relieving the worker before he becomes really bored, or by giving him adequate time to

---

[1] See Vernon, H. M., and Bedford, T. *Rest-pauses in Heavy and Moderately Heavy Industrial Work*. Industrial Fatigue Research Board, Report Number 41. London, His Majesty's Stationery Office, 1927.

overcome whatever wearisomeness he acquired during his work day. It has been predicted that the laborer will soon have a four-hour or five-hour day. If this prophecy comes true, there should be little boredom in industry, for work does not become monotonous when repeated for the first few times, but only after prolonged performance of it. Short work days also afford time regularly for doing some other things of interest, and so enable the individual not only to work for a living, but also to live.

3. Week-ends and Holidays

Week-ends and holidays may serve effectively both of the objectives of leisure. Such periods of respite from toil can be sufficiently refreshing to maintain the individual's original adjustment to his work. Week-ends and holidays, however, provide ordinarily more leisure than is necessary to overcome the evil effects of work, and are desired mainly because they enable the doing of things that cannot be done on work days. The enjoyment of such occasions is suggested by the extent to which people await and plan for an annual holiday. Every employee needs to be a free man for a day or two each week; those who are not tend to grow morbid, and to question whether life with its restrictions is worthwhile.

4. Annual Vacations

A yearly vacation makes possible the doing of things that cannot be done in any of the shorter periods of leisure, and is eagerly sought and often highly enjoyed for this reason. The benefits that can be derived from an annual vacation are so great that everyone should have several weeks of free time every year.

Many school children live under greater restrictions during the summer months than during the school year, and so their vacation is of little avail to them. Communities that cannot provide activities of interest to the children in the summer certainly ought to conduct school throughout the year. They might make the study periods shorter and the recreational periods longer. Many grown-ups likewise fail to profit materially from a vacation because of having no satisfactory way of spending it. They may, when on vacation, be heard saying, "I'll be glad to get back to work."

Although annual vacations are highly enjoyable to those able to spend them advantageously, they cannot take the place of daily, week-end or holiday leisure. These more frequent, although more limited, leisure periods for doing things of interest are fundamental to mental health. An annual vacation must *supplement* the briefer and more frequent leisure periods; it must not *supplant* them.

CHAPTER XIV

GETTING THE INDIVIDUAL IN TOUCH WITH NATURE

"The earth was made so various, that the mind
Of desultory man, studious of change,
And pleas'd with novelty might be indulg'd." [1]

NATURE affords man many striking changes from his other experiences. Its vastness contrasts with the limited indoor space; its serenity, with the disquietude of much urban life. Nature is also infinite in its variety. The world consists of innumerable kinds of things, and each kind is made up of myriad gradations between wide extremes. The surface of the earth is irregular and consists of different substances, each highly varied. No two mountains, valleys or waters are alike, and the differences in rocks are as numerous as are the rocks. Vegetation everywhere affords a varied spectacle, and to the traveler a continual change of scenery. Trees differ from each other in detail or kind, and flowers vary in color, form, size, texture and scent. Fruits and vegetables are of more than one taste and texture, and differ in every other quality. The species of animal life are countless, and the individuals within each species differ in every trait. The sky has many wonders, and those who be-

[1] Cowper, William. *The Task*, Bk. 1, l. 506.

hold them delight in the view and find it refreshing. The colors of the earth and sky are myriad, and the most general tones are varied throughout their extent; no leaf or mountain has but one hue, and the sky has the rainbow and the sunset. Differences in light and shadow render objects still more various. Nature's sounds also are diversified, and vary throughout their duration. All animals, winds, waters, and thunder far and near have different voices, and seldom is a tone of nature a monotone. No imitator would attempt to mimic the entire range of sounds. To each of the special senses of man nature affords pleasing diversity.

To the variety of impressions afforded by a thing observed from one position, change of impression is added as one observes it from different points. And when a person approaches something or recedes from it there is a continual change of impression.

Many of the things of nature are varied to such a degree that they contrast with each other. Some flowers are poised on firm stalks, and others sway on delicate stems. The day brings light and shade, and the night gives us darkness and the light of the moon. We have also the low notes and the high notes of living creatures, trickling and gushing streams, and we have the stillness before the storm. For a number of sharply contrasting scenes, take a trip through the Dakota prairies, through the Canadian Rockies, down the coast by boat, visit the California forests, come back through the Arizona desert, stop at the Grand Canyon and return over the plains.

Nature gives variety also in the form of action. Floating clouds, flashing lightning, swaying trees, blazing fires, erupting volcanoes, and the various activities of the animal kingdom, especially those of man, give richness to the view. The diversity of the attributes of nature is amazing, but the diversity of nature in action is infinite.

Nature, moreover, undergoes continuous change. The clouds unceasingly alter their form, color or movement, and many other scenes of nature change while you look. The seasons shift in a cycle in which they bring in turn the green, the red, the gold, the gray and again the green, and give us the rain and the snow. All living things grow for a time, and so differ from day to day in the process of maturing, and the earth undergoes continual modification. Throughout nature's range, things in time are transfigured. Ever changing, ever new, how could nature tire one!

Much of what I have said on the subject of variety in nature can be summed up by the following quotation.

"Certainly no one can say that life on this planet is stale and monotonous.... In the first place, there is the alternation of night and day, and morning and sunset, and a cool evening following upon a hot day, and a silent and clear dawn presaging a busy morning, and there is nothing better than that. In the second place, there is the alternation of summer and winter, perfect in themselves, but made still more perfect by being gradually ushered in by spring and autumn, and there is nothing better than that. In the third place, there are the silent and dignified trees, giving us shade in summer and not shutting out the warm sunshine in winter, and there is nothing better than that. In the fourth place, there are flowers blooming and fruits ripening by rotation in the different months, and there is nothing better than that. In the fifth place, there are cloudy and misty days alternating with clear and sunny days, and there is nothing better than that. In the sixth place, there are spring showers and summer thunderstorms and the dry crisp wind of autumn and the snow of winter, and there is nothing better than that. In the seventh place, there are peacocks and parrots and skylarks and canaries singing inimitable songs, and there is nothing better than that. In the eighth place, there is the zoo, with monkeys, tigers, bears, camels, elephants, rhinoceros, crocodiles, sea lions, cows, horses, dogs, cats, foxes, squirrels, woodchucks and more variety and ingenuity than we ever thought of, and there is nothing better than that. In the ninth place, there are rainbow fish, sword fish, electric eels, whales, minnows, clams, abalones, lobsters, shrimps, turtles and more variety and ingenuity than we ever thought of, and there is nothing better than that. In the tenth place, there are magnificent redwood trees, fire-spouting volcanoes, magnificent caves, majestic peaks, undulating hills, placid lakes, winding rivers and shady banks, and there is nothing better than that. The menu is practically endless to suit individual tastes, and the only sensible thing to do is to go and partake of the feast and not complain about the monotony of life." [2]

In addition to giving a variety of sensory impressions, nature also makes one think beyond the thing perceived. A river slowly moving down a winding course with green and shade on either side suggests relaxation and many related ideas. The drooping branches of the weeping willow give the thought of melancholy. A flower, by virtue of its structure, may suggest a stately building, a graceful animal, a modestly furnished home, a serene sky or a gay person. The scenes produced by a tempest imply power, and may give the individual imaginary experiences in which he, like the storm, exercises great might. All nature is suggestive, and so the variety it affords is not limited to the diversity it presents to the senses, but takes in also the things it suggests.

[2] Lin Yutang. *The Importance of Living*, p. 280. New York, The John Day Company, 1937. Used by permission of the publisher.

GETTING THE INDIVIDUAL IN TOUCH WITH NATURE 135

Many of the aspects of nature are not discordant, but are harmoniously related; they differ, and still they agree. And it is not simply nature's variety that we enjoy, but its *unified variety*.

Nature is, of course, often very harsh and cruel; but although it may vex you exceedingly, it never bores you.

> "The earth never tires,
> The earth is rude, silent, incomprehensible at first, Nature is rude and incomprehensible at first,
> Be not discouraged, keep on, there are divine things well envelop'd,
> I swear to you there are divine things more beautiful than words can tell." [3]

Since nature has an inexhaustible store of highly pleasurable novelties, it is possible to refresh the lives of people by bringing them into contact with nature.

The individual frequently inhabits richer surroundings than he realizes, and, when this is the case, his lack of observation of the things about him may be due to the fact that he is not very observant. Some persons notice only huge mountains, deep gorges and great waterfalls; others notice little effects of every sort: the return of a bird, the opening of a bud or the work of ants. To see and to hear much it is necessary not only to have eyes and ears, but also to look and to listen. The person who observes well enriches his life greatly in a momentary glance or in a short stroll; he sees millions of details that to others go unobserved. Such a person can often feel as did Sydney Smith when he said, "How nature de-

[3] Whitman, Walt. "Song of the Open Road," Stanza 9. From *Leaves of Grass, The Modern Readers' Series*. New York, The Macmillan Company, 1926. Used here by permission of the publishers.

lights and amuses us by varying even the character of insects; the ill-nature of the wasp, the sluggishness of the drone, the volatility of the butterfly, the slyness of the bug!"

Failure to observe nature may be due to lack of knowledge in regard to nature. Through their courses in nature study, schools do much to make children more observant. It may be due also to the need of heeding incessantly the call to labor, to ill-health or to malnutrition. Mark Twain said, "Nothing improves scenery like ham and eggs." Failure to be observant of nature and interested in it may be due also, as the following quotation implies, to the human tendency to undervalue reality in comparison with the fictions of the mind.

"It is amazing that no one ever questions the truth of the story of a lost Paradise. How beautiful, after all, was the Garden of Eden, and how ugly, after all, is the present physical universe? Have flowers ceased to bloom since Eve and Adam sinned? Has God cursed the apple tree and forbidden it to bear fruit because one man sinned, or has He decided that its blossoms should be made of duller or paler colors? Have orioles and nightingales and skylarks ceased to sing? Is there no snow upon the mountain tops and are there no reflections in the lakes? Are there no rosy sunsets today and no rainbows and no haze nestling over villages, and are there no falling cataracts and gurgling streams and shady trees? Who therefore invented the myth that the 'Paradise' was 'lost' and that today we are living in an ugly universe? We are indeed ungrateful spoiled children of God.

"A parable has to be written of this spoiled child. . . . He came to God and complained that this planet was not good enough for him, and said he wanted a Heaven of Pearly Gates. And God first pointed out to the moon in the sky and asked him if it was not a good toy, and he shook his head. He said

GETTING THE INDIVIDUAL IN TOUCH WITH NATURE 137

he didn't want to look at it. Then God pointed out to the blue hills in the distance and asked him if the lines were not beautiful, and he said they were common and ordinary. Next God showed him the petals of the orchid and the pansy, and asked him to put out his fingers and touch gently their velvety lining and asked if the color scheme was not exquisite, and the man said, 'No.' In his infinite patience, God took him to an aquarium, and showed him the gorgeous colors and shapes of Hawaiian fishes, and the man said he was not interested. God then took him under a shady tree and commanded a cool breeze to blow and asked him if he couldn't enjoy that, and the man replied again that he was not impressed. Next God took him to a mountain lake and showed him the light of the water, the sound of winds whistling through a pine forest, the serenity of the rocks and the beautiful reflections in the lake, and the man said that still he could not get excited over it. Thinking that this creature of His was not mild-tempered and wanted more exciting views, God took him then to the top of the Rocky Mountains, the Grand Canyon, and the caves with stalactites and stalagmites, and geysers, and sand dunes, and the fairyfinger-shaped cactus plants on a desert, and the snow on the Himalayas, and the cliffs of the Yangtse Gorges, and the granite peaks of the Yellow Mountains, and the sweeping cataract of Niagara Falls, and asked him if He had not done everything possible to make this planet beautiful to delight his eyes and his ears and his stomach, and the man still clamored for a Heaven with Pearly Gates. 'This planet,' the man said, 'is not good enough for me.' 'You presumptuous, ungrateful rat!' said God. 'So this planet is not good enough for you. I will therefore send you to Hell where you shall not see the sailing clouds and the flowering trees, nor hear the gurgling brooks and live there forever till the end of your days.' And God sent him to live in a city apartment." [4]

To bring into contact with nature, or with reality in general, an individual who undervalues reality we must

[4] Lin Yutang. *The Importance of Living*, p. 277. New York, The John Day Company, 1937. Used by permission of the publishers.

refrain from teaching sweet falsehoods in regard to things remote, and to acquaint the individual with the fact that distant pastures seem greenest.

Getting the individual in touch with nature is often a very simple matter: a matter of providing a window with a view. And such a window can enrich the simplest home. All living creatures like the outdoors. A dog or cat when indoors often leaps upon a chair at a window, and a child makes fingerprints on the glass. A window that adds a landscape to a home is frequently far more essential from the standpoint of diversity than is an extra room. The view of merely one tree silhouetted against a short stretch of sky gives much enrichment to a home. People who spend a large part of their time indoors need greatly the refreshing experience of gazing out upon nature, and of seeing the changes wrought by the weather and the seasons. Such persons often value a window that gives them an exceptional landscape more than they do the rest of the house.

The desire for a window with a view is not simply a desire to see the outdoors. A room without a window gives a pent-up feeling. Such a feeling is not pleasant; we desire, on the contrary, a feeling of freedom from restraint. Persons who have been confined to a room without a window have experienced a desire to push out the walls. A spacious view enables the mind to range at large. The desire to be unrestricted and the desire for variety combined make very urgent a window with a view.

Getting people in touch with nature is a simple way of providing variety for nature abounds on every hand. And when you get them in touch with her, you get them in touch with a refreshing friend.

CHAPTER XV

PROVIDING ACTIVE AND PASSIVE RECREATION

ACTIVE recreation consists in doing things; passive recreation consists in merely receiving impressions. There is need for both forms. People generally find more pleasure in recreation in which they play an active part than they do in that in which they are passive. Many persons, capable of doing so, would rather paddle a canoe than ride along idly; would rather take the part of a character in a play than watch another act the part. This is because such activity involves the exercise of skill, ingenuity or talent, and so provides feelings of personal worth. The use of leisure for maintaining a sense of personal worth is especially important today because many laborers consider their work degrading. There are, of course, many persons whose occupations involve creative work or other forms of self-expression, and who, therefore, do not need leisure activity for maintaining self-respect. But there are millions of people whose tasks are very simple, and who need, and need greatly, recreational activity which calls for ingenuity or skill. If people in general pursued recreational activity requiring special ability, it would be asked not only, "Where do you work?" but also, "What do you do aside from your regular occupation?" Then the individual whose work is of a simple kind would be saved from feelings of humiliation by his proficiency in his leisure activity.

Many forms of active recreation are enjoyed also because they involve physical activity. Man, being constructed to use his limbs, finds doing so, like giving expression to any other native tendency, satisfying. The urge toward gross bodily activity is especially apparent in the child, to whom the most unreasonable request is that he sit still. The desire for physical activity, although waning at the approach of middle age, exists throughout life, and is a significant factor motivating various types of activity on the part of adults. Sports of all kinds, the different manual arts, gardening, shoveling snow or mowing a lawn may give pleasure because they involve the use of the body. The more sedentary the regular work, the more enjoyable is recreation involving physical activity.

Active recreation, in addition to being pleasurable, makes the individual self-refreshing. The more proficiency he develops in forms of diversion, the less dependent he becomes upon other persons or things to give direction to his thoughts and actions. Those who have no capability for anything are paupers in recreation. Speaking of such persons someone has said, "They forever cry, 'Tickle and entertain me or I'll die.'" There is no more pathetic spectacle than that of a person unable to find amusement for himself—one so unresourceful that he can bear neither momentary silence nor occasional solitude. Such a condition does not exist when people are skilled in recreations.

Recreation that involves "trying the hand at things" has the further advantage of uncovering talent which with further development may contribute something of value. No one will ever know how much potential ability on the part of men and women has been wasted because of an unawareness of it. A recreational program that provides wide choice of activity should bring out latent ability.

Recreation cannot always be classed as active or passive solely on the basis of what is done. A person who listens to music simply for the sensory impressions that it affords is in a passive state; the one who studies the art of the composer while listening to a performance of his composition is, to that extent, in an active state. Likewise, reading a novel purely for enjoyment is passive activity, while studying any book critically is an active process.

Although everyone needs active recreation, the range of experience would be greatly limited if people could have only recreations of this type. An elderly person could have few athletic or theatrical experiences, and none could view a landscape, listen to music or read simply for idle amusement. Everyone is greatly limited in the active forms of recreation that he can have and needs passive forms as supplementary experiences. Passive recreation may be enjoyed also because of an interest in witnessing perfection. Athletes often leave their own fields and travel many miles to see the performance of other and better athletes, and any pianist would leave his instrument to hear a Paderewski. But if the individual studies the art of the performer while observing him, he plays, to that extent, an active part.

Even though recreation to be enjoyed need not necessarily be of the participating type, some previous participation in a form of recreation is sometimes essential to its fullest enjoyment as a spectator. Those who have performed in music and those who have taken part in athletics may enjoy such performances on the part of other persons more than they would if they had never taken an active part in such recreation.

People in general have more recreation in which they are passive than recreation in which they are active. Seeing novel things in the outdoors or theater, reading of the unusual, or hearing new performances over the radio is a repeated experience of many persons. But doing something out of the ordinary is a far less frequent diversion of the masses.

People have a preponderance of passive recreation not because they prefer it, but because active recreation is not equally available to them. Recreation is sponsored primarily by private enterprise, and those who provide it must, in order to continue operation, be able to make a profit. Most active recreation requires so much space and equipment per person that private enterprise cannot provide it on a paying basis.

Because of the failure of private enterprise to provide active recreation for people in general, there has developed a sentiment in favor of establishing means of diversion through community enterprise, and much recreational space and equipment have been made available by governmental action. Cities are building parks. Originally, municipal parks were designed to provide only scenic areas, but today the tendency is to build and equip them so that they provide diversified recreation, especially recreation in which the individual plays an active part. This is obvious when one considers that many municipal parks provide for children such play facilities as sandpiles, water sprays and pools, seesaws, slides, swings and traveling rings; for young people, areas for such sports as tennis, volley ball, baseball, football and swimming or skating; and for oldsters, opportunities for horseshoe pitching, fly-casting, archery and for playing croquet.

Many of the county and state governments and the national government also have established parks which afford active, as well as passive, recreation for many people. The original purpose in choosing sites for such parks was, as in designing city parks, to provide scenic beauty, but most parks are now intended to serve also as playgrounds. In providing for such enjoyments as picnicking, swimming, fishing, dancing, hiking, climbing, canoeing, or motorboating these various parks constitute valuable means of recreation.

There is a strong interest in the conservation of forests and in reforestation not only for material ends, but also for recreational purposes. To add to the attractiveness of existing wooded regions, the forest service is setting aside an area in each forest to be left in its natural condition. These areas are called "primitive areas," and they provide sharp contrast with everyday experiences.

One of the most notable advances in providing outdoor space for recreational purposes is the establishment of marine parks. Until recently there was little restriction put upon lining the waterfronts of cities with docks, with manufacturing establishments and with warehouses; but the exploitation of waterfronts for industrial purposes is being somewhat curtailed in the interest of creating scenic shores. Many of the rivers and lakes of cities are polluted so that they cannot be used much for water sports. Some cities have established sewage-disposal plants. There is a definite, although a very slow, trend toward keeping, in this way, the streams and lakes from being polluted.

Camps originally were all on a commercial basis, and so were available only to those able to meet the financial requirements. Recently camp life has been made available to many others, primarily to children and young people, through governmental action, private philanthropy, and through the Y.M.C.A. and other such organizations. Many welfare boards, especially those directing children's and young people's organizations, are doing much to extend opportunities for camp life. As a result, a significant number of children and young people in particular spend their vacation at camps, and find their vacations refreshing.

Most communities provide at least some playgrounds for school children, and there has been a continuous insistence upon more school playgrounds for children of all ages. This insistence has, however, met with very limited success. The enlargement of playgrounds in congested school districts, where land values are high, has seemed almost prohibitive, and, as a result, such schools have very inadequate space. In 1929, twenty per cent of the elementary schools in the United States, and about fifty per cent of the city high schools had neither playgrounds nor athletic fields.[1] In the purchase of new school sites today many cities, however, are providing for more ample recreational grounds, and thus reveal a trend

---

[1] Steiner, Jesse Frederick. *Americans at Play*, p. 22. New York, McGraw-Hill Company, 1933.

toward more adequate play space for public school children.

Many communities provide considerable indoor space and equipment for recreational purposes. In some cities, school buildings are opened evenings for adults. Where this is done one may see on a single evening different members of the community participating in plays and concerts, working at crafts, playing games, dancing, swimming or engaging in other forms of athletics, and participating in open forum discussions. Thus the school sometimes becomes a many-ringed circus, but one in which the actors are members of the community and often outnumber the spectators. In many communities churches, city halls and special community centers are made available for recreational purposes. In all cities of note there are good libraries; libraries that are well-stocked, and in which books are displayed, shelves opened for browsing, story hours for children conducted to make them aware of interesting books available, and in which suggested reading lists or standard readers' guides are made available to all. And for many sparsely settled places, traveling libraries are provided.

Thus, much recreation, like education, is now provided on a public basis, and, as a result, people are having the kind of recreation for which they have the greater need: activities in which they can participate, rather than spectacles they must watch. Governmental participation in providing recreation extends over almost a half century, but is most noteworthy today. During the last several years the Works Progress Administration has been co-operating with local governments in providing work for the unemployed. Many persons on relief are now repairing, improving and constructing parks, playgrounds, swimming pools and public recreation facilities of many kinds; others are planning and directing recreation programs. The joint activity of the Federal and local governments now extends into more than half of the counties of the United States, and there is practically no form of physical, social or cultural recreation that is not carried on in this way. The Works Progress Administration, through its director of recreation, Eduard C. Lindeman, has rendered certain real services to the cause of recreation by carrying into a great many communities principles that only some of the more advanced had recognized and that still fewer had put into operation. It has emphasized in theory and practice that recreation has important value to the individual and to the community; that recreation should be primarily of the participating type, and should consist of physical, social and cultural pursuits; that local communities, and larger communities when necessary, should put recreation in general, as it has already put libraries and schools, on a public basis. Through community enterprise we can readily provide sufficient opportunities for the employment of leisure hours and for the proper balance between active and passive recreation.

CHAPTER XVI

ENCOURAGING THE PURSUIT OF HOBBIES OR DIVERSIFIED INTERESTS

Any form of active recreation to which spare time is given repeatedly is a hobby. Hobbies differ, therefore, from other forms of active recreation in frequency of pursuit, rather than in kind. Who should have a hobby? The degree to which a form of recreation engrosses the mind depends somewhat on how deep a person goes into it; the more one penetrates what one does, the more gripping it becomes. By reverting to a thing again and again one often bores into it to such an extent that it grips the attention more than do unspecialized interests. Some persons have work that is sufficiently engrossing to keep their minds adequately employed or sufficiently diverted from unpleasant things. Persons who do not have such work need hobbies, and can profit more from them than they could profit from spreading their attention widely.

Everyone needs a sense of personal worth, and such satisfaction is more likely to result from a high degree of proficiency in one activity than from ordinary proficiency in a number of different activities. By turning again and again to the same thing, more than common ability can usually be developed. The person whose work does not sustain his self-respect therefore needs a hobby, as does one whose occupation is insufficiently engrossing to be enjoyed or to divert his mind from unpleasant things. The longer such a person devotes himself to his hobby the more it becomes a representation of him, and, consequently, the more he becomes interested in building it up as something with which he can proudly identify himself. Many a person's relish of his hobby is due primarily to his capability therein.

People who have work that must be turned over in old age to younger persons have great need of hobbies upon retirement. This applies to a continuously increasing number of persons, because the age for retiring is being lowered. A retirement plan that provides only subsistence and does not afford opportunity for doing something overlooks a great human need. Much unhappiness of the retired is due to inadequately or improperly employed minds and to a loss of a sense of personal worth. A good hobby is needed to prevent such distressing conditions.

Elderly people, upon being retired or widowed, often take up residence with relatives, and, in doing so, sometimes create a severe in-law problem; a problem that, as I said, is frequently due to boredom. Persons who upon being taken into the homes of relatives have hobbies can amuse themselves and be interesting to other members of the home, and hence can avoid creating tedious relationships. Everyone should realize that a hobby is important in old age, not simply from the standpoint of escaping drearisome hours, but also from the standpoint of keeping oneself from making life dreary for those in whose home one may need to take up residence. If there is anything worse than being bored, it is to bore other persons. A hobby is as much of a protection against the latter of these evils as against the former.

Hobbies for the retirement period must be acquired before the retirement age is reached, because old persons are not facile in acquiring new interests. One of the wisest provisions for retirement consists in laying up in the early years a store of interests from which a hobby may spring when needed, or in developing early a hobby that persists to the end of life.

Those whose work is sufficiently engrossing, those who get feelings of personal worth from their occupations, and those who are able to continue their occupations throughout life can profit from hobbies for the same reasons for which the less fortunate in these respects profit, but they have no urgent need for hobbies.

What constitutes a good hobby? To be enjoyed, a hobby must be chosen not because of its prestige or popularity, but because one likes it. Love for a hobby should be the first consideration in adopting it. Another essential of a good hobby is that its possibilities for development be unlimited. A hobby that must eventually be discontinued because it can be carried no further should seldom be chosen in preference to a more lasting one. A good hobby is also one that is convenient, and that is, for persons in moderate circumstances, inexpensive. Some hobbies have social value, and such hobbies are especially enjoyable because everyone likes to feel that he counts for something in the lives of other persons —that he is not living in vain. An example of a hobby that may have all of these points in its favor is writing. There is for every person a topic that is of interest to him and that he can never exhaust. Writing is also a very convenient hobby because it can be carried on anywhere and in any moment of leisure. Writing requires much reading, but good libraries are available to many people. Writing, furthermore, has possibilities of contributing something to human knowledge.

Should a hobby·be related to the individual's work or wholly different from it? The more anyone's recreational activity differs from his occupation, the greater is the change of experience it provides and the more it enables him to forget his work and whatever unpleasantness there may be about it. Largely for this reason, some persons adopt unusual hobbies. Unusual hobbies are, however, adopted also for the purpose of receiving more attention than could be got from a familiar line of activity, such as stamp collecting. Persons who have strange hobbies often get greater recognition for the nature of what they do than for their proficiency in doing it. They may be regarded as queer, but even such attitudes toward them is recognition. The great diversion and esteem experienced when engaging in a strange hobby often make it very satisfying.

Although hobbies wholly different from work give definite satisfaction, hobbies closely related to work also have decided values. They are less likely to interfere with work. There is always the danger of becoming so interested in a hobby as to neglect one's work; but hobbies closely related to work make for capability in it, and are easily developed because the work, conversely, has a bearing on the hobby. A hobby in line with work, moreover, can be pursued without embarrassment. The person whose hobby is foreign to what he does in his occupation often feels apologetic when caught devoting time to it. The one whose hobby has kinship to his work can say with truth that his hobby helps him in his occupation.

But to look askance at someone engaged in a pet pursuit is often wholly unjustified. People need to be educated to an acceptance, in many cases, of the value of a hobby for its own sake. Hobbies closely related to work have a further value. They suggest interest in work; hobbies wholly different from work may suggest lack of interest in it. And obvious interest on the part of an individual in his work is necessary to create interest on the part of others in what he does or confidence in him. The person who is known to like his work ordinarily needs to say little to convince others as to the worth of what he does. Hobbies similar to the occupation and hobbies different from the occupation have advantages over each other. The type of hobby that should be chosen depends upon the individual and upon his occupation.

Frequently a hobby to be pursued at all must of necessity be closely related to work. This is because many occupations are of such a nature that those who engage in them need to grow in their work if they wish to continue in it. An individual having such an occupation cannot have also an interest wholly unrelated to it. He must choose a hobby that has a bearing on his career, or get along without one.

How the individual rides his hobby is as important as is the nature of his hobby or the extent to which he rides it. A person who, with writing as a hobby, asks everyone again and again to read or listen to what he writes, or who has a literary group put him unwillingly on a program, is not a pleasing character. A similar remark may be made in regard to the pursuit of any hobby; he who talks his hobby or about it continually destroys himself socially. But one should not, as a rule, urge the individual who abuses his hobby to discontinue it; rather, one should give him a riding lesson or have him read something on how to carry on a hobby. Frequently the need of a hobby is so real and its benefit to the individual so great that his personal well-being requires that he continue it with undiminished application.

In addition to the need of hobbies on the part of some, there is need of diversified interests on the part of others. Everyone should have, as previously stated, a somewhat rounded life; everyone should have physical, cultural and social activity. The person whose occupation or hobby does not provide such experiences needs other interests that do so.

Some persons try to pursue several hobbies and many other diversified activities in addition to an occupation. But those who strive to encompass the universe in their lives ultimately break down their nervous systems and never achieve anything but variety. Edison was once asked why he accomplished so much when other men accomplish so little. He said, "I don't do more than other men do. The point is I do one thing, and other men do many things." When questioned in regard to diversion, he replied, "My work is my recreation." But just as too much diversification frequently results in an unfruitful life, so also the doing of one thing to the exclusion of everything else is dangerous. "Shun not toil to make yourself remarkable by some one talent,—yet do not devote yourself to one branch exclusively." Everyone should seek to attain what is for him, from the standpoint of accomplishment and from the standpoint of enjoyment, the proper balance between concentrated and diversified activity.

CHAPTER XVII

ALLOWING FREEDOM IN LEISURE HOURS

THE enjoyment of leisure necessitates considerable freedom of choice in recreation. But most people are not free in the spending of their leisure; they may be governed by various factors in taking up diversions. Some find it necessary to devote their spare time to the furthering of their occupational interests. A man may on many a day spend all of his free time playing golf, not with a partner of his choosing, but with a business prospect or with a superior to whom he feels he must cater. He may also join a church other than the one he prefers and attend services regularly because he finds that in doing so he gets some of his best clients. Babbitt confessed that he never in his life did anything he wanted to do. The aspiration to climb socially, like the economic motive, leads many to seek the company of someone of note rather than the companionship of an enjoyable person. This desire also prompts many such husbands and many such wives to require their mates or their children to do likewise. So frequently is this fact portrayed in the comic strip that it need not be dwelt upon here. Fashion and convention may also lead the individual into spending his leisure in one way when he prefers doing something else. Whether a woman may ride a bicycle or whether anyone may attend a social function dressed as he prefers to dress depends on what fashion or convention says about it. Club membership is another factor that may involve the forfeiting of much freedom in leisure hours. When a member of a group sets a pace in entertaining that others follow because they feel they must, the social club becomes a chain-gang.

A very significant hindrance to spending leisure as one chooses is lack of privacy. In the home it is often necessary to talk with someone or to undergo the conversation of other members of the household, to reply to telephone calls or calls at the door, or to listen to a radio program when you prefer, for the time being, to read or think. No one can be said to have a home in the complete sense of the word who does not have a room of his own. Still another hindrance to freedom in leisure hours is the imposing of a standardized scheme of recreation. The prescribing of leisure activity, however rich may be the experiences provided, defeats the purpose of leisure, which is freedom to do what one is interested in doing.

> "Say, Dora! tell me, by yon placid moon,
> If called to choose between the favored pair,
> Which would you be,—the bird of the saloon
> By lady-fingers tended with nice care,
> Caressed, applauded, upon dainties fed,
> Or Nature's DARLING of the mossy shed?" [1]

Persons whose spare time is not at their own disposal, but is dominated in one way or another, soon come to look upon work as a relief from leisure. Every husband, wife, parent, business associate and friend should display an emancipation-proclamation sign that reads, "You shall

[1] Wordsworth, William. "The Contrast: The Parrot and the Wren."

not be unnecessarily enslaved by me during leisure hours."

To profit by freedom in leisure hours, people must be given a variety of recreational activities from which to choose. And offerings must be made with regard to different interests on the part of different ages and on the part of persons of each age. There must be made available a broad range of physical, of social and of cultural activities. Desire on the part of many persons for recreational activity of a cultural nature has always been recognized, but such recreational activities have never been made available to the extent desired. More and more opportunities for self-improvement are, however, being extended to people in all occupations. Educational institutions, through their evening schools and correspondence study departments, offer a large variety of courses to adults. There are also industrial organizations that provide such services for their employees, or encourage and financially support them in taking up evening school classroom work or correspondence study courses offered by educational institutions. Many adults who take up study with instructors trained and experienced in the teaching of adults say with deep feeling that they obtain more enjoyment from their study than they could obtain from anything else to which they might devote their leisure. All should have opportunity to devote leisure to learning, as well as to other things of interest.

Many of those in charge of recreational activity of one type or another know the value of freedom to choose from broad offerings, and strive to make such choice possible. Librarians have found that a variety of reading material and freedom to select books and magazines stimulate interest in reading, and so they display books, prepare printed lists of books, and aid readers personally in making selections rather than attempt to direct their reading. Similarly, the recreational division of the Works Progress Administration, as stated previously, maintains a good distribution of physical, social and of cultural activities, and provides broad opportunities in each of these types of recreation. It furthermore is imbued with the conviction that recreation must be governed by free individual choice. The balanced recreational program provided by this agency of our government and the free choice of activity that it encourages are especially noteworthy because there is today a tendency on the part of some other nations to limit the field of recreation and to put much dutifulness into the activity provided.

A wide offering of wholesome recreational activity and freedom to choose the activity desired do not, however, assure wise use of leisure. An amazingly large number of persons ruin their leisure and the leisure of those with whom they mingle by the kind of recreation they choose or into which they drift; they do many things during their spare time that are far more unpleasant than the most disagreeable work could be, and they become a blight to all with whom they mingle.

To prevent such abuses of leisure, choice of activities must be made intelligently. Schools should develop in the early years an interest in the better forms of recreational activity. They can do so most effectively by aiding children in acquiring some proficiency in desirable activities to which they might later devote their leisure. Usually skill is necessary for the enjoyment of any form of activity that involves self-expression. Without some adeptness in a leisure pursuit, it can be as uninteresting as the most routine work. But high proficiency in recreational activity is not essential to making it interesting. Just enough information or skill in a form of activity to enable the individual to feel that he can perform somewhat successfully in it is often enough to get him to take it up as a leisure pursuit. Preparing for the use of leisure has always been recognized as an objective of the school. Because most work today is unskilled and because leisure is increasing, vocational training is now less important for the majority of people than is training for enjoyment of leisure. Training for lesiure is, however, vocational training for those who may later make their leisure pursuits their vocation.

Some limitation of freedom in the spending of leisure is essential to gregarious life; it is only in solitude that the individual will ever be able to do as he pleases with his spare time. But since spontaneity in the doing of things is a factor in their enjoyment, unnecessary curtailment of freedom in the choice of leisure activity should be carefully avoided, and every effort should be made to enable people to have the kind of socially acceptable leisure activity they desire.

CHAPTER XVIII

MAKING IT POSSIBLE TO MEET PEOPLE

MEETING other people—people that one knows and unfamiliar people—is a means of obtaining new experiences. Those well known may be refreshing because they speak and act freely; new acquaintances because they provide novelty of appearance, speech and action. Making a new acquaintance or meeting a familiar one may afford not only new impressions, but also opportunity for talking, and so the variety that meeting people gives is a variety of impression and of expression. Either type of experience can be as effective as the other in engaging the mind or in diverting it from anything unpleasant.

Contacts with people are often more effective in employing the mind and in keeping it from distressing circumstances than other experiences could be. This is due partly to the fact that conversation makes a continuous demand upon the individual's attention. Isolation, even in a place in which the material stimulation is great, may permit mind-wandering in the form of brooding over trouble, but companionship as a rule holds the mind in constant communication. This is suggested by the fact that when with someone, the individual frequently finds the time going quickly; when alone, he may spend a year in a day.

Human contacts may be effective in occupying the mind and in keeping it from unpleasant things also because man is intensely interested in his kind. He is primarily a social being. Many people mingle as widely as circumstances permit and find their human contacts the chief attractions of their lives. " 'Man is preeminently interested in man; nay if you look strictly to it, there is nothing else interesting.' How inexpressibly comfortable to know our fellow creature; to see into him, understand his goings-forth, decipher the whole heart of his mystery; nay, not only to see into him, but even to see out of him, to view the world altogether as he views it." [1] They who are amid the best of natural scenery always maintain sufficient interest in people to shift their attention to a human being in a landscape. Many persons who long to live in the heart of nature because they love nature and because they are racked by the tumult of the city are, nevertheless, held to the city by the attraction of fellow-beings. They feel, as did Walt Whitman when he wrote:

I

"Give me the splendid silent sun with all his beams full-dazzling,
Give me juicy autumnal fruit ripe and red from the orchard,
Give me a field where the unmow'd grass grows,
Give me an arbor, give me the trellis'd grape,
Give me fresh corn and wheat, give me serene-moving animals teaching content,
Give me nights perfectly quiet as on high plateaus west of the Mississippi, and I looking up at the stars,
Give me odorous at sunrise a garden of beautiful flowers where I can walk undisturb'd,

[1] Carlyle, Thomas. *Essay on Man.*

Give me for marriage a sweet-breath'd woman of whom I should never tire,
Give me a perfect child, give me away aside from the noise of the world a rural domestic life,
Give me to warble spontaneous songs recluse by myself, for my own ears only,
Give me solitude, give me Nature, give me again O Nature your primal sanities!
These demanding to have them, (tired with ceaseless excitement, and rack'd by the war-strife,)
These to procure incessantly asking, rising in cries from my heart,
While yet incessantly asking still I adhere to my city,
Day upon day, and year upon year O city, walking your streets,
Where you hold me enchain'd a certain time refusing to give me up,
Yet giving to make me glutted, enrich'd of soul, you give me forever faces;
(O I see what I sought to escape, confronting, reversing my cries,
I see my own soul trampling down what it ask'd for.)

2

"Keep your splendid silent sun,
Keep your woods O Nature, and the quiet places by the woods,
Keep your fields of clover and timothy, and your corn-fields and orchards,
Keep the blossoming buckwheat fields where the Ninth-month bees hum;
Give me faces and streets—give me these phantoms incessant and endless along the trottoirs!
Give me interminable eyes—give me women—give me comrades and lovers by the thousand!
Let me see new ones every day—let me hold new ones by the hand every day!
Give me such shows—give me the streets of Manhattan!

Give me Broadway, with the soldiers marching—give me the
  sound of the trumpets and drums!
(The soldiers in companies or regiments—some starting away,
  flush'd and reckless,
Some, their time up, returning with thinn'd ranks, young,
  yet very old, worn, marching, noticing nothing;)
Give me the shores and wharves heavy-fringed with black
  ships!
O such for me! O an intense life, full to repletion and varied!
The life of the theater, bar-room, huge hotel, for me!
The saloon of the steamer! the crowded excursion for me!
  the torchlight procession!
The dense brigade bound for the war, with high piled military
  wagons following;
People, endless, streaming, with strong voices, passions,
  pageants,
Manhattan streets with their powerful throbs, with beating
  drums as now,
The endless and noisy chorus, the rustle and clank of muskets, (even the sight of the wounded,)
Manhattan crowds, with their turbulent musical chorus!
Manhattan faces and eyes forever for me." [2]

The movement of the population from rural districts and small towns to cities is, of course, due to economic forces, to the conveniences of urban life and to a desire to be identified with the city rather than with the small town or the farm, but it is due also to a desire to be within view of and in contact with people to a greater extent than is possible in more sparsely settled localities. "It is people that makes places." Novelists and playwrights know that most people are interested less in events than in the characters around which events take

---

[2] Whitman, Walt. "Give Me the Splendid Silent Sun." From *Leaves of Grass*, New York, The Macmillan Company, 1928. Used here by permission of the publishers.

place, and so they deal not simply with things happening, but with the individuals to whom they happen. Newspapers realize that no news is interesting unless there is a person in it, and that the sale of a paper is increased by the inclusion of a society section or personal column, especially when it carries photographs. Edwin C. Hill gave, over a period of several years, radio talks that he referred to as "The Human Side of the News," and later published his talks under this title. Educators have observed that all subjects are enlivened when taught in reference to people; that even the abstractions of philosophy can be made palatable by stressing the human side, as is done in Durant's *Story of Philosophy,* and that history is remembered when taught in relation to human beings instead of in relation to dates. Educators have observed also that classroom groups can be too small to be interesting to students and instructor, or too large to enable them to get acquainted, and that correspondence study lacks the personal touch found in the classroom.

To enjoy human contacts people must have personal attraction for each other. The wretchedness of being with unsympathetic persons can be more severe than the wretchedness of being unwillingly alone. Young people usually prefer persons of their own age to persons either much older or younger than they; children prefer children of their own age, and there is a tendency for adults to seek to be with others who have interests similar to theirs. Persons are most interested in other persons of opposite sex. To a man or woman the company of someone of the other sex may be most interesting. Much of the diversion that people enjoy involves the sex element, and a recreational program that excluded the sex factor entirely would make a limited appeal. Sex stimulation, however, frequently diverts the mind excessively; it often operates to the extent of distracting the individual from his work when he should be giving his attention to it. But this is so in the case of those whose sex desire is always aroused and never gratified, rather than in the case of those who have achieved sex adjustment. Despite the strength of the sex desire, people often prefer to be with members of their own sex.

The extent to which people may meet depends upon the location of their residences and upon where they work. So does the extent to which they shift about determine the company that people may have. Today the majority of people live in densely populated areas, and there is considerable change of residence and of employment. The amount of leisure is also an important factor underlying the meeting of acquaintances and the making of new ones; the greater leisure of today means greater opportunity for coming in contact with others. Leisure, furthermore, keeps people from growing dull to the extent of becoming retiring or from being unstimulating when in the company of others. Places where people may assemble in large numbers are also needed for gregarious experiences. Such places should, furthermore, be equipped for enabling people to engage in group activity which brings them into closer relationships than do passive amusements. Many of the parks and beaches of today serve these purposes well. Dining in public places, and going about with others in private conveyances or using public transportation facilities, also bring people together. Adequacy of clothing is a significant factor determining the extent to which persons mingle with others.

Most people with quite small incomes can now have suitable clothes, to some extent a variety of clothes, for different occasions. Many persons have been to the same places, have listened to the same radio programs, or have seen the same films, and so have common experiences, which provide material for conversation. Convention is becoming less rigid in respect to strangers speaking with each other. Although this greater freedom is subject to grave abuse, it need not be dangerous if people are prepared for it, and it does have the good effect of affording many lonesome strangers the enjoyment of getting acquainted. Big affairs, such as receptions, band concerts, community picnics or public celebrations enable everyone to touch elbows with others. People have always enjoyed the diversity of stimulation of large gatherings. Organizing people may make it easier for them to get together. Membership in an organization brings into the company of others some who would otherwise seldom meet anyone. But this means of furthering social contacts has shortcomings; it tends to limit the individual's range of acquaintance to the members of the organization. It should, therefore, be supplemented with big community affairs or other means of bringing unacquainted people together, such as an occasional joint meeting between different organizations or open-house on the part of a group. Getting acquainted involves more than merely coming together. At almost any meeting there should be a definite program for having people mingle. Without some management there is danger, for instance, that the Smiths upon seeing the Joneses at a party will rivet themselves to the Joneses; that Henry and Helen, who come together to a dance and go home together, will also dance together the entire evening. Such practices enable the persons concerned to meet about as many people at a social function as they would have met if they had had a private meeting at home. To prevent individuals or couples from staying paired throughout the whole evening, hostesses or directors of social functions may employ various means for getting people to mingle. They often pair persons arbitrarily. But in doing so, frequent change of partners or a very brief partner program is necessary to avoid the possibility of somewhat uncongenial persons "getting stuck" with each other. There are people who realize that in entertaining groups it is quite unwise to have just persons who see each other every day, and so when planning a social function they aim to have a guest or two unfamiliar to the other guests. A strange person or couple can do wonders toward enlivening a gathering. Some bridge clubs are made up of an odd number of couples, so that each hostess has to contribute a fresh pair of faces to the occasion when it is her turn to have the party. A good social leader also does much to bring people into conversation by directing the talk.

There are persons who withdraw from others. Many people avoid crowds, and greatly limit the number of persons they take into close relationship. They usually do so, however, because their social stimulation is excessive or because they are ill-adapted. All young people in particular have a very strong desire for human contacts. Those who always tend to remain alone experience frustration, and the frustration of any strong desire creates a distraught mind. Some maladjustments are due to feelings of inferiority for which personal or social factors, usually social factors, are responsible. Other maladjustments are due to an unwillingness to contribute toward the welfare of others, or to profit from them. There are many individuals who look upon another human being as a child looks upon a parent: as someone to contribute to their welfare and happiness, and not as someone with whom they may go along for mutual benefit. The prevention of maladjustment of this type necessitates training children to contribute unto others as they would have others contribute unto them. Continuous seclusiveness must, therefore, not be regarded a normal condition. The normal desire of man is to be with man, and everyone needs now and then the refreshing experience of meeting a stimulating person whom he knows well and of making a new acquaintance.

CHAPTER XIX

AFFORDING OPPORTUNITY FOR CHANGE OF SCENE

VARIETY may be had by going to different places, and people often seek to refresh their minds through change of scene. They may, for the pleasure of novelty, visit the homes of other persons, go on week-end trips to near-by places or take long journeys. Often the more unusual the new scenes, the more interesting they are. People who live in green fields find the city's huge crowds, its hustle, its incessant clamor and its flashing lights most attractive; people who live amid skyscrapers are drawn by the open spaces. And anyone may enjoy going to one place or another not simply because of the newness of the destination, but also because of the ever changing series of impressions enroute.

Generally the main attraction of foreign travel is the strangeness it provides: different speech, different coins, different clothes, different food, different architecture and different attitudes and customs. Going abroad wrenches anyone out of the humdrum of his customary life, and, however trying foreign travel may become, it is usually preferred occasionally by most people to the comfortable uniformity of a sleepy existence. The desire for taking a long trip is often intense. There is a song which tells, in substance, that a train-caller, after announcing a train for a number of stations and all points west, said to himself in a subdued voice, "There comes, I believe, a traveling salesman. He's probably going all the way to the Coast," and then muttered, "but I never go anywhere." Later the train-caller announced a train for other stations and all points east, and then to himself remarked, "There comes a honeymoon couple. They're headed for Niagara Falls, I'll wager," and mumbled, "but I never go anywhere." Next he announced a south-bound train, and uttered, "There come the police with a prisoner for Leavenworth, I suppose. That fellow looks angry. But why should he be mad; he's getting a trip out of it." Then the train-caller was accidentally injured fatally, and his dying words were, "Well, after all, I'm going somewhere!"[1] Although this story overdraws people's desire to travel, the desire that it emphasizes is real. Traveling occasionally may do much to further mental health.

There is also novelty experienced in the manner of going places. Some means of locomotion involve bodily activity not had in one's occupation. Walking provides physical change from sitting at a desk or in a lounge, and such physical change not only benefits the body, but also refreshes the mind. Walking is, moreover, the simplest means of obtaining change of scene; one can always go walking and thereby be freed from a monotonous view. Cycling, like walking, provides physical change from work, and is often preferred to walking simply because it is a different means of going about. The bicycle is a means of locomotion accessible to many because it is inexpensive. Motoring is a very satisfactory means of travel. The development of the automobile and good

[1] Hart, Lorenz. "All Points West." Music by Richard Rogers.

roads make available many places that could not be reached in any other way, and enable people to travel together at their convenience, in comfort and at low cost. Furthermore tourist camps and camping grounds, well-marked roads, travel information bureaus and the distribution of maps make motoring a very satisfactory means for people in general to obtain change of scene. Taking a trip by train, boat or airplane is enjoyed when it constitutes a new means of travel. Riding in a motor boat, in a sail boat, in a canoe, in a carriage, or riding a horse may, likewise, be enjoyed because they are novel means of transportation.

Some people spend many week-ends and summer vacations at the same lake, where they have a cottage; others want every vacation to be different and won't tie themselves down to one place. But the former, like the latter, although to a less degree, seek change of scene.

It is not only in leisure time, but also when pursuing occupations that change of scene is had and enjoyed. All persons, except housewives and others who work where they live, have considerable change of impression in going to and from their work. This is so especially in the case of those who live in large cities, where different routes may be taken and where a beaten path, although often annoying, never becomes very monotonous. Some persons in carrying on their work go about considerably from place to place, and so have change of scene throughout the day. Young people have new surroundings when they go away to college; teachers, by leaving their communities in vacation time and attending summer school in another place. Many people in all occupations go to conventions, or take up short courses for a week or longer at educational institutions. People who in pursuing occupational interests are taken to new scenes find recreation in their work.

Although many people are mobile in occupational or in leisure hours, many others, for one reason or another, have a very limited range of movement. Some cannot go far, either a-foot or by means of a conveyance, because they lack adequate clothing or because they are unable to procure transportation; others cannot do so because of the incessant demand made upon them by their occupations, as in the case of some housewives. Steps are taken, however, to rectify such conditions. Children and young people are formed into organizations and are provided places of recreation and transportation at a low cost. As a result, many who otherwise could not go far beyond their premises, have worthwhile experiences in new places. More community action should be directed toward making it occasionally possible for persons of all ages to have change of scene.

CHAPTER XX

AFFORDING PRIVACY FOR READING AND INDEPENDENT THOUGHT

READING is a means of extending experiences; so is independent thought, which ranges from daydreaming to creative thinking. New impressions, new ideas and new emotions can be had by turning to the printed page or by thinking by oneself. Such employment of time satisfies now some wants, now other wants, but always the want for variety. Real experiences often fall far short of the experiences desired, and so these means of extending the scope of life are necessary for preventing tedium. Everyone who is able to read and to think well can thereby make his existence fuller, and, consequently, more interesting.

Reading, in addition to providing variety of experiences, gives peace to a distraught mind by diverting it from the cause of anxiety. The printed page is one of the most effective and most widely used means of getting away from disturbing and unalterable circumstances.

Reading and independent thought may provide variety by affording society in solitude. A person with well-selected books can in a way meet all kinds of people, for a good library makes the reader an inhabitant of any nation and a contemporary of any age and brings the wisest, the wittiest and the tenderest across his threshold. Books are not satisfactory substitutes for all direct personal contacts, but they are valuable means of supplementing real human relationships. What a narrow life man would have if he could know the thoughts and feelings of only those whom he actually met! Contacts with others through the printed page have an advantage over direct human relationships in that the persons between the covers of books may suit one's mood of the hour; they stand ready to come and ready to go at one's bidding. Everyone occasionally chooses a book in preference to an available companion for diversity of thought, and many do so regularly. Anyone, especially the child, can have companions also through independent thinking and may have them at will.

Reading and independent thought may provide variety also by giving trips to those unable to travel. There are books that take one roaming, and thus afford pleasing change of scene. On the pages of books of travel new lands rise, new seas roll, and spring may be had in winter. Travel by means of reading does not afford the degree of satisfaction obtained from actual travel, but most people cannot take physically the trips they desire. Everyone is limited in the places to which he can actually go, and many, for one reason or another, cannot travel in person at all. But a library provides an open road to all geographic and human scenes, and enables everyone to go abroad at home. It is possible to travel far and wide also simply through independent thought.

A very effective way in which reading and independent thought provide variety is by making all emotions articulate. One of the functions of literature is to depict the whole of human action—the dark and wild passions as well as the bright and the gentle. In doing so it presents various situations, characters and incidents. The good novelist and the good dramatist give such a broad picture of the life of man that their works create a wide range of intense emotional effects. And there is much interest in such reading material.

The mind engaged in independent thought may conjure up episodes as exciting as those experienced through reading, but it ordinarily does not do so, because imaginary experiences usually lack the novelty of the occurrences in books. This is because the drama that the individual creates is based on his own experiences, while the drama enacted on the pages of a book is based on experiences which may differ considerably from those of the reader.

Anything experienced in reading or in independent thought may be appreciated because it is recognized as an inevitable outcome of a series of other events, rather than because it is exciting. An event may even be disliked because of the emotion it arouses, while it is liked because of its intellectual implication. People who enjoy stirring events may be emotionally impoverished, but this is not true of those who enjoy them for the aptness with which they depict life. Most people, however, have such inadequate emotional lives that they enjoy the excitement of a stirring event, even though they may appreciate it primarily for its intellectual implication.

Still another way in which reading and independent thought afford variety is by enabling the individual to undergo change of identity. It is monotonous to many people to always be themselves. But through reading and independent thought the individual can for a change acquire an existence other than his own. It is a common source of pleasure to persons of all ages, especially to children, to imagine that they are what they are not. Every youngster has crawled and growled like a bear, whinnied like a horse, flapped his wings like a bird, hopped like a frog, puffed and made motions suggestive of an engine starting on its run, or has imagined himself being a parent, a grocer or a teacher. Adults, likewise, frequently project themselves into other persons or animals. We have, for example, in athletics, the "Bears," and in aviation we have the "Eagles." At masquerades individuals, by means of costume and affectation of tone or movement, pretend to be other persons or even animals. The most common change of identity on the part of the adult is that of becoming another person. His imagination is often sufficiently fertile to enable him to identify himself with a character in a story, and thus to become a cowboy and ride a strawberry roan, to run for a touchdown, to woo or to be wooed, or to delight or sway an audience. Tired of his customary existence, the individual may change in imagination to an existence other than his own, and thus avoid the monotony of being always himself. The desire for change of experience is a common cause of change of identity.

Change of identity is usually change to an existence in which the individual plays a part superior to that of his real existence, and so provides a feeling of importance, as well as variety. Other wants also may be gratified through this form of adjustment, and a thwarting of a combination of wants constitutes a very powerful drive toward change of identity for their gratification. But a thwarting of the want for variety alone and a desire to obtain a more varied existence may be sufficient to cause change of identity.

Although reading and independent thinking of the wish-fulfillment type often benefit the individual by giving him change of experience and other satisfactions, both are subject to abuse. Such reading and thinking afford only representations of things; they never provide anything real, and so the satisfactions they give are inadequate for life. Airy substitutes for reality are, moreover, attainable without effort, and so the individual may devote himself to creating phantoms of the things he desires, rather than to exerting himself to obtain the things themselves. The more he leaves the real world, the more he loses orientation to it, and so the more difficult it becomes for him to make the adjustments to reality that successful living requires.

Much daydreaming, with the aid of the printed page or without it, is a result of dissatisfaction with reality, but it is also a cause of further dissatisfaction with it. Phantasy is an alluring exaggeration of what it represents, and so it makes the real world seem pallid or hard. The greater the individual's aircastles, the more disheartening does he find the actual world. All aircastles are, moreover, flimsy structures that crumble as soon as they are set up. The relapse that the individual suffers upon the termination of a daydream is often far more disheartening than the moments spent in phantasy were bracing. As a means of wish-fulfillment, daydreaming is of benefit to the individual when engaged in as a diversion, rather than as a main pattern of life. All need some opportunities for reading and thinking of the wish-fulfillment type, but all must guard against being alienated by the wanderings of their minds from the real world.

Although reading and independent thought are often of the uncontrolled wish-fulfillment type, they are, of course, not primarily of this character. Much literature is read because it is informative. Desire for information is one of the chief motives underlying reading. And independent thought often consists in creative thinking. The novelty of information received in reading and the novelty of an idea that flowers in independent thinking may be most refreshing. Informative reading and creative thinking may, however, be enjoyed not simply because they are refreshing; they may be enjoyed also, among other reasons, because of the sense of personal worth that acquiring information and exercising originality give. Of the satisfactions that may be got from reading and independent thought the satisfactions that informative reading and creative thinking give are, to many persons, the greatest and most enduring.

Reading and independent thought require privacy. Too frequently persons are denied seclusion. Cramped home conditions, which are very common, make it difficult for members of families to read or simply to devote their thoughts to matters of personal interest. When dining in a public place many persons, desirous of privacy, take recourse to the newspaper for maintaining it. This is one of the many things often done in order to have solitude in society. Men and women of prominence when preferring to be alone must continually fight a human tide that beats incessantly against their privacy, and that would sweep it away completely. Many prominent persons are swept into a sea of social activities. Those who have been denied privacy for reading or independent thinking have often cried out,

> "Give me, kind Heaven, a private station
> A mind serene for contemplation."

Everyone must, of course, expect to have his privacy invaded occasionally for the privilege of invading that of others. But a greater understanding of the need of privacy would result in fewer intrusions upon it. Such an understanding would also result in better feelings on the part of persons toward each other because it would make for a realization that to fly from, need not mean to hate, mankind.

CHAPTER XXI

ENLARGING EXPERIENCE THROUGH POETRY

LITERARY works of every kind are transcripts of life, real or imaginary, and so serve to broaden experience. All poetry enlarges experience in that it is different from prose in form, and much poetry does so in that it involves more unusualness of thought and manner of expression than prose generally does. It is as true of many poets today as it was true of many poets when the following stanza was written, that,

> "First, to surprising novelties inclined,
> The bards some unexpected objects find,
> To wake attention and suspend the mind.
> A cold dull order bravely they forsake;
> Fixed and resolved the winding way to take,
> They nobly deviate from the beaten track." [1]

The poet may be original in thought because he deals with something unfamiliar to most people, because he deals with a commonplace fact that is generally overlooked, because he views a familiar thing differently than do most people, because he sees familiar things in new relationships, or because he puts much emphasis upon the

[1] Vida, Marco Girolamo. *Art of Poetry*, Bk. II, l. 58. See Albert S. Cook, *The Art of Poetry*, p. 81. New York, G. E. Stechert and Company, 1926.

thoughts he presents. A poet may see "a world in a grain of sand and a heaven in a wild flower."

"I believe a leaf of grass is no less than the journeywork of the stars,
And the pismire is equally perfect, and a grain of sand, and the egg of the wren,
And the tree-toad is a chef-d'œuvre for the highest,
And the running blackberry would adorn the parlors of heaven,
And the narrowest hinge in my hand puts to scorn all machinery,
And the cow crunching with depress'd head surpasses any statue.
And a mouse is miracle enough to stagger sextillions of infidels." [2]

In manner of expression also, poetry generally has more unusualness than does prose. Unusualness of the language of poetry over that of prose does not necessarily mean, however, that unusualness is more appropriate to poetry; often it means simply that the poet is more skilled in the art of expression than is the writer of prose. The language of poetry tends to exceed that of prose in novelty of words, in variety of sentence structure, in imagery and in figurativeness. Said a poet in speaking of his art:

"With figures numberless your story grace
And everything in beauteous colors trace." [3]

Poetry, no less and often more than prose, gives contrasting thoughts and feelings.

[2] Whitman, Walt. "Song of Myself," stanza 31. From *Leaves of Grass,* Copyright 1928, The Macmillan Company. Used here by permission of the publishers.
[3] Boileau-Despréaux, Nicolas. *Art of Poetry,* Canto 3, l. 286. See Albert S. Cook, *The Art of Poetry.* New York, G. E. Stechert and Company, 1892.

> "More pleased are we to see a river lead
> His gentle streams along a flowery mead,
> Than from high banks to hear loud torrents roar,
> With foamy waters, on a muddy shore." [4]

Unexpectedness, within the limits of plausibility, is also an attribute of poetry, and underlies interest in it.

> "The mind is most agreeably surprised,
> When a well-woven subject, long disguised,
> You on a sudden artfully unfold,
> And give the whole another face and mold." [5]

> "I am monarch of all I survey,
>   My right there is none to dispute;
> From the centre all round to the sea,
>   I am lord of the fowl and the brute.
> Oh, solitude! where are thy charms
>   That sages have seen in thy face?
> Better dwell in the midst of alarms,
>   Than reign in this horrible place." [6]

> "Whenever Richard Cory went down town,
>   We people on the pavement looked at him:
> He was a gentleman from sole to crown,
>   Clean favored, and imperially slim.

> "And he was always quietly arrayed,
>   And he was always human when he talked;
> But still he fluttered pulses when he said,
>   'Good morning,' and he glittered when he walked.

> "And he was rich—yes, richer than a king,
>   And admirably schooled in every grace:
> In fine, we thought that he was everything
>   To make us wish that we were in his place.

[4] *Ibid.*, Canto 1, l. 166.
[5] *Ibid.*, Canto 3, l. 55.
[6] Cowper, William. From "Verses."

"So on we worked, and waited for the light,
  And went without meat, and cursed the bread;
And Richard Cory, one calm summer night,
  Went home and put a bullet through his head." [7]

As some of the above poetical passages reveal, and as the following couplets say, the thoughts of poetry may arouse various emotions.

"Happy he who in his verse can gently steer
From grave to light, from pleasant to severe!" [8]

"Hear how Timotheus' varied lays surprise,
And bid alternate passions fall and rise!" [9]

Poets, like prose writers, arouse images of various senses, but they tend to do so more extensively. In the following poem we get, on the one hand, a very noticeable mental picture of bodily movement (kinesthetic image) from the rhythm of the lines. It is interesting to say these lines repeatedly simply for the feeling or riding the waves that the rhythm gives.

"I must go down to the seas again, to the lonely sea and the sky,
  And all I ask is a tall ship and a star to steer her by,
And the wheel's kick and the wind's song and a white sail's shaking,
  And a grey mist on the sea's face and grey dawn breaking.

"I must go down to the seas again, for the call of the running tide
  Is a wild call and a clear call that may not be denied;

---

[7] Robinson, Edwin Arlington. "Richard Cory." From *The Children of the Night*. New York, Charles Scribner's Sons, 1914. Used here by permission of the publishers.
[8] Boileau-Despréaux, Nicolas. *Art of Poetry*, Canto 1, l. 74.
[9] Pope, Alexander. *An Essay on Criticism*, Part 1, l. 374.

And all I ask is a windy day with the white clouds flying,
And the flung spray and the blown spume, and the sea-gulls crying.

"I must go down to the seas again to the vagrant gypsy life,
To the gull's way and the whale's way where the wind's like a whetted knife;
And all I ask is a merry yarn from a laughing fellow-rover,
And quiet sleep and a sweet dream when the long trick's over." [10]

We get kinesthetic images not only from the rhythm of this poem, but also from "the wheel's kick" and from "the white sail's shaking." Other words of this poem give us visual and auditory images and images of the skin senses.

Variety in manner of expression is had also in the rhythm of poetry. The unit of rhythm is called a "foot." It consists of one or more accented and of one or more unaccented syllables. Feet differ in the number and in the sequence of their accented and unaccented syllables. Each of the following lines has four feet, and the foot-pattern of each line differs from the foot-pattern of the other lines.

The splen|dor falls| on cas|tle walls,|
I a| light ca|noe will| build me| ...
And the sheen| on their spears| was like stars| on the sea,|
Make no deep| scrutiny| into her| mutiny.|

[10] Masefield, John. "Sea-Fever." From *Collected Poems by John Masefield*. New York, The Macmillan Company, 1928. Used here by permission of the publishers.

ENLARGING EXPERIENCE THROUGH POETRY

The rhythmic patterns are called, respectively, iambic, trochaic, anapestic and dactylic.

Poems are written on one or the other of these rhythmic patterns. This is done in order that they, like everything else in art, may have distinctiveness, and, more fundamentally, because there is a human interest in the repeated recurrence of the same rhythmic pattern, and a joy in being able to recognize it. But the rhythm of a poem usually does not adhere rigidly to a single pattern. In cases in which it does, it has a sing-song effect like that of a nursery rhyme. Some of the ways in which rhythm in good poetry is varied consist in substituting occasionally a different foot, omitting occasionally a foot or a beat of a foot, changing the time, introducing pauses. In the following example it will be seen that the main rhythm of the poem "Evangeline" is changed by omitting a beat in the last foot of each line and in the third foot of the second line.

"This is the | forest pri|meval. The| murmuring|pines and the| hemlocks,|

Bearded with| moss and in| garments| green, indis|tinct in the |twilight,"|

An occasional change in rhythm is enjoyed especially because it comes unexpectedly. The poet accustoms you at the outset to his basic rhythmic pattern, and so you look for a continuation of it in every foot and are surprised upon coming to a deviation from that rhythm. Unexpectedness is a significant factor in the enjoyment of varied rhythm.

A departure from the chief rhythmic pattern is often made not only for the sake of variety, but also for the purpose of precision of expression and for the purpose of making the main rhythmic pattern less obvious and thus increasing the joy of recognition. But, whatever the motives in varying the rhythm, the resulting diversity gives enjoyment.

The purpose of poetry, like that of other literature, is not simply to make life interesting, but that is one of its purposes, and it serves that purpose well. From the standpoint of making life interesting we may say of the poet, and of the artist in prose as well:

> "The rich variety he sets to right
> Cloys not the mind, but adds to its delight." [11]

More of the attributes of poetry are experienced when a poem is heard than when it is read silently. For this reason the radio, to which we shall give consideration in a later chapter, has possibilities for increasing the enjoyment of poetry.

[11] Vida, Marco Girolamo. *Art of Poetry,* Bk. III, l. 64.

CHAPTER XXII

ENLARGING EXPERIENCE THROUGH VISUAL ART

ALL arts have this in common: they are means of enlarging experience. The experiences that the visual arts give are superior to those given by the verbal arts in that they are more concrete. A picture is worth a thousand words if it is more real. Visual art, furthermore, affords pleasing change from verbal language because it is markedly different from it. Since it is vivid and gives change from verbal language, visual art can interest any mind, and divert effectively a mind misemployed.

Art gives variety not only by enlarging experience, but also by being in itself varied. In any work of art there is repetition, but usually the repetition involves variety. In painting and in other visual arts, a given design or objects of a certain form may recur in a progression of sizes, in different colors, or in one color of various degrees of saturation or brightness. All visual arts also involve variations in spacing. In a composition, persons or things are usually put at unequal distances from each other; parallel lines are spaced unequally. Groups of persons or things in a composition are, as a rule, made up of various sizes; an artist generally forms groups of two and three, rather than groups of two and two.

Alignments in art vary. Large objects in a room are put so that their lines are parallel with the lines of the room; but for the sake of variety (and informality as well) chairs are placed to form transitional lines; tables and other things to form contrasting lines. Objects for the room or for the mantel and pictures for the wall are chosen so that their upper parts are not wholly in line with each other. There is, however, a definite tendency in modern art to maintain a relationship of horizontals by lowering, for example, book cases and coffee tables, and thus to prevent feelings of upness and downness.

Art is made interesting also through variations in light, shade and color. Passing from one of these elements of art to another is enjoyed because of the change experienced in doing so. When one is satiated with a color, change to another color or to something without color is pleasant. A room that shows a variety of harmonious colors is more interesting than a room in which color is unvaried.

A composition is sometimes varied, as the furniture of a room is sometimes arranged, to achieve contrast. Curved lines are turned in opposite directions, and dissimilar objects are put in juxtaposition. Next to each other are put light and shade, bright and dull or warm and cold colors, a fretted and a plain surface, or empty and filled spaces. The contrasting elements in art are, however, not without a harmonious background; they consist of small contradictory things overshadowed by larger things in accord with each other.

The variety of art, like that of verbal language, often involves unusualness in either matter or manner of expression. And the message or the language of visual art is frequently most engrossing. Unusualness of thought in art is sometimes expressed in cartoons. Most cartoons are exaggerations of the things they portray, and, for this reason, make a wide appeal. Many persons dislike certain cartoons, such as those in which human frailties or deformities are portrayed, or in which one man hunts down another, but their eyes are nevertheless attracted by the unusualness that such cartoons depict. It is difficult to keep one's attention from something out of the ordinary however distasteful it in itself may be. Unusualness in manner of expression is a goal of every artist, and much of the beauty of art consists in unusualness attained through originality. But sometimes beauty is ill-advisedly sacrificed for novelty because of an overwhelming desire to be striking.

It is not simply variety that is enjoyed, but *unified variety;* a variety in which all of the parts have a common characteristic and contribute toward the same effect. Unity in the visual arts, as in language, is necessary to avoid confusion or contradiction in expression, and it is also a factor in the enjoyment of art. The mind always seeks for something common to things that are different, and is ever pleased to find a unifying characteristic. Without unity there is no art. But an extremely uniform composition in art, as in verbal language, is monotonous, and such a composition may even go unnoticed. It may represent or suggest something accurately, but not interestingly. Some variations within the limits of uniformity are always necessary. "The art of composing well," said Hogarth, "is the art of varying well."[1]

Variety is had in all arts through variations in sym-

[1] Hogarth, William. *Analysis of Beauty,* Ch. III.

metry. Symmetry in anything is pleasing, but complete uniformity of corresponding parts is often monotonous, and suggests too mechanical a balance. To create interest some variation in symmetry is made. The two sides of a woman's dress are usually not identical; complete symmetry is prevented by means of a skirt pocket, a sash tied to one side, an ornament to the right or left on the waist, or her hair may be parted on a side; she may wear a bracelet on one arm, or a tilted hat.

A variation in symmetry does not destroy symmetry, but rather accentuates it. The higher the boughs in a tree, the more are they usually inclined upward. But some boughs do not follow this general tendency, and the exception calls attention to the rule. A variation in symmetry, therefore, not only gives variety, but makes the symmetry felt.

Art represents things as they seem, and thus makes them appear more varied than they really are. Distant objects are made smaller, fainter in color, and more vague in outline than near objects, and the farther end of a building is made smaller than the near end by making the lines converge as they recede.

"It is a constant rule in composition in painting to avoid regularity. When we view a building, or any other object in life, we have it in our power, by shifting the ground, to take that view of it which pleases us best; and in consequence of this, the painter, if he is left to his choice, takes it on the angle rather than in front, as most agreeable to the eye, because the regularity of the lines is taken away by their running into perspective, without losing the idea of fitness; and when he is of necessity obliged to give the front of a building, with all its equalities and parallelisms, he generally breaks (as it is termed) such disagreeable appearances, by throwing a tree before it, or the shadow of an imaginary cloud, or some other object that may answer the same purpose of adding variety, which is the same with taking away uniformity." [2]

The artist, of course, represents things as they seem largely in order that his composition will appear to be a good likeness, but he is never unmindful of the pleasurable variety that certain perspectives afford.

Art enlarges experience not only by providing new impressions; it does so also by giving you something to do. And valuable as are the impressions of art for interesting or for diverting the mind, those ends are attained most fully through creation. The infant delights in making marks, in shaping sand or clay into forms and in wielding a paint brush; the trained hand of the adult does not quickly weary of producing art. The Eskimo finds joy of expression and relief from the tedium of the long arctic nights by carving on walrus tusks creatures he has known. By carving dog sleds, reindeer and polar bears, he carves his way to contentment. A very fundamental law in respect to human needs is that man must have something to do, and the most enjoyable activity is the *self-expressive* type. The urge to activity will not be daunted. The reason some people talk all the time is that they have nothing else to do. The way to cure a garrulous person, and at the same time make him happy, is to give him another means of self-expression. The aim of art education from the standpoint of mental health is not simply to train a few for giving pleasure to the many, but also to train many for self-amusement.

[2] Hogarth, William. *Ibid.*

CHAPTER XXIII

ENLARGING EXPERIENCE THROUGH MUSIC

THE subject of music is of interest to us here because of its recreational value. Music, since it creates emotional states, is an effective means of bringing about change of experience. It provides pleasurable diversion during periods of inactivity, facilitates enjoyment of many performances such as dancing, in which it is involved, heightens the effect of dramatizations and moving pictures, and gives pleasing background or atmosphere for various activities. As a means of recreation for many people, music ranks high. Shakespeare said that it is preposterous not to know of the value of music for refreshing the mind.[1]

Music gives variety not only by enlarging experience, but also by being in itself well varied. The melody of most music consists of ever varying changes in pitch. It is only the most elementary forms of music that have melodies as simple as that of "Yankee Doodle" and of "Pop Goes the Weasel." The melody of primitive man was of this sort; it was short, restricted to two or three tones, and the same phrase was constantly repeated. Musical themes today are varied and prolonged so as to form a highly elaborate melody. In many musical selections of the great composers, themes are as extended and

[1] Shakespeare, William. *Taming of the Shrew*, Act III, Sc. 1, l. 9.

varied as the mind can grasp. Likewise, the rhythm of good music does not consist of square-cut repetition of tunes as does that of the simplest march music, but of repetitions that are varied in time, in force, in key and in many other ways that tax the ear in attempting to recognize the melody.

Melody and rhythm to be enjoyed must give not simply variety, but variety that is unified; the tones must be connected systematically so that they will have a definite form. Definite form, or unity, is essential to all arts; no unity, no art. But unity without variety, in music as well as in other art, is as unsatisfying as variety without unity. Simple dance tunes with their sharp accents and short intervals have the highest unity, but their lack of variation makes them monotonous. That which is enjoyed in the sequence and repetition of any musical tones is not unity, not variety, but unified variety.

The variety of music is not simply the variety of melody and rhythm, but also the variety of combined harmonious tones and of change in combination of tones. The combining of different voices, of different instruments, of one or more voices and instruments, change in combination of voices and instruments, and the simultaneous singing or playing of two parts of a musical composition give richness to music. The possibilities of providing different combinations of harmonious tones and change in combination of tones are great because there are different voices and many different standard instruments. The usual ways of combining different tones are even enlarged upon occasionally by the improvising of a musical device, such as a saw or the rungs of a chair for tonal effect. Any melody and rhythm, captivating at first, will sooner or later lose freshness, but combined harmonious tones have a complexity that does not soon tire. A fine bit of harmony is pleasing because it consists of tones that blend and that differ.

Music in any of its forms often delights the ear with successive or simultaneous tones that contrast. High and low, loud and soft, rapid and slow, mellow and harsh, or greatly varied and wholly uniform tones follow or accompany each other in all interesting music. Contrast is provided also in balanced programs. A western song heard after a Hawaiian selection, or a brilliant orchestral work by Ravel heard after a Beethoven symphony, may be enjoyed, not simply because of itself, but also because it is extremely different from what went before. Usually contrasting numbers, rather than similar numbers, are given in succession on any program.

Is novel or familiar music preferred? A familiar composition is often enjoyed because you can recognize it, because you can anticipate each part when the preceding part is played, because you can hear your anticipation carried out, and because you observe more in it than you would if it were less familiar. Ability to recognize a piece, to anticipate its parts from moment to moment, to hear your anticipation fulfilled and to observe details give self-satisfaction. It is obvious that no significant degree of such experience can be had from hearing a new composition.

A musical composition is enjoyed not simply because of the successive tones it provides, but also because of the form of the composition as a whole. In any art, the parts possess value not only in themselves, but also in their contribution to the development of the whole. In music it is more difficult to get the effect of the elements combined than in the visual arts because in music the elements are perceived successively, while in the visual arts they can be taken in simultaneously. One must, therefore, be well informed concerning a musical selection to get the effect of the elements combined; so familiar that when one part is heard the other parts can be recalled. A new musical composition can seldom be recalled sufficiently to be perceived in its entirety.

Music is a language, and, to be effective, this language, like verbal language, must be understood. How clear is the language of music? Emotions are normally expressed through words, tones, looks, postures and gestures. Vocal music may involve all of these attributes of an emotion and may express an emotion with a definiteness somewhat equal to the definiteness with which it is expressed in speech.[2] Instrumental music can express only the tone of the voice, and can but approximate the tone; it cannot reproduce it. A musical instrument is, therefore, more limited than is the singing voice for expressing an emotion. Certain emotions may become associated with, and, as a result, be suggested by, music of a certain type, but the association between emotion and type of music does not become so definite that an instrument can express an emotion as distinctly as can the human mechanism. A new composition of calm music might represent to one person the sadness of a disappointed lover; to another, the tranquillity of conjugal love.

---

[2] For expressing the harsh emotions the speaking voice is more effective than is the singing voice because it takes on more of the harsh qualities, when needed, and because it is freer to slide up and down the scale. For expressing the mild emotions the singing voice is superior because it is smoother.

For expressing definite ideas, music in itself is far more inadequate than it is for expressing emotions. It cannot differentiate clearly between a calm man, a still evening landscape and the blithe flow of a brook, nor between the fury of an enraged man and the rush of a mad cataract. The inadequacy of music for expressing emotions and ideas distinctly is acknowledged in the practice of distributing to an audience explanations of program or descriptive music. The emotional tone and meaning of a composition often become known as the composition becomes familiar, and a familiar composition that is understood may be greatly preferred to a novel one not understood.

Music is usually heard, not apart from other pleasurable experiences, but with them. As a result, those other experiences often become so definitely associated with particular pieces of music that they are brought to mind upon the repeated hearing of that music. Much of the enjoyment of music is the enjoyment of remote experiences that the music supplies.

"All music is what awakes from you when you are reminded by the instruments,
It is not the violins and the cornets, it is not the oboe nor the beating drums, nor the score of the baritone singer singing his sweet romanza, nor that of the men's chorus, nor that of the women's chorus.
It is nearer and farther than they.[3]

Familiar music that brings back pleasurable experiences of yesterday has a value that novel music does not have, and is preferred when it does so.

[3] Whitman, Walt. "A Song for Occupations," Stanza 4. From *Leaves of Grass*. Copyright, The Macmillan Company, New York, 1928.

Music is enjoyed largely because of the sensory pleasure it gives, and the newness of a composition may add to its sensory delight. From the standpoint of auditory impressions only we can often say, in the words of Pope:

> "Novel lays attract the ravish'd ear
> But old, the mind with inattention hears."

Although the enjoyment of music goes beyond an enjoyment of sensory impressions, sensory impressions are fundamental to it, and so a degree of novelty, other things being the same, increases the pleasurableness of music.

In speaking of the recreational value of music it is necessary to specify whether one has reference to listening to music or to producing music. Listening is a passive means of enjoyment if the hearer merely receives auditory impressions and a few memories that the music suggests. It is, in a way, an active means if he sees each phrase as a consequence of what went before, and as a necessary antecedent of what follows. But actually to produce music is to play a wholly active part; and active recreation, as I said in respect to visual art, is more satisfying than passive recreation. Everyone needs a variety of impressions and a variety of means of self-expression. To train people in musical appreciation and to neglect training them in musical expression is to overlook the enjoyment of active recreation as against the passive type.

CHAPTER XXIV

ENLARGING EXPERIENCE BY MEANS OF RADIO BROADCASTS

WE ARE interested here in the subject of radio broadcasts insofar as they free individuals and groups from isolation and make possible the sharing of experiences in general. Radio is the greatest means of enlarging life that has been devised since the invention of the printing press. It has remarkable possibilities for freeing people from the dullness of an otherwise narrow environment, and for giving them things they enjoy. By means of radio broadcasts, information and entertainments can be carried from any part of the world to any other part, and at a low cost per person. For giving out news, the radio, although inferior to the press in that it is less detailed and makes no record of news, is superior to the press in that it is quicker; broadcasts go over the air in less time than newspapers can be distributed widely. The immediacy of news is always a factor underlying its enjoyment. The listeners can, moreover, have reports of an event as it progresses, and so enjoy the suspense and surprise that are had by the onlookers.

The value of the radio for education depends much on how the school of the air is conducted. Any learning process is more than a listening process; it requires saying, writing or doing what one would learn; it requires knowledge and correction of errors; and it requires, in the case of young children, immediate personal recognition of accomplishment. Subject matter should be individualized in accordance with the personal needs and interests of everyone. A teacher who has direct contact with the learners is in a better position to apply these principles of education than is the speaker before the microphone. The schools of the air are devising ways of putting these principles into operation, but they cannot do so to a sufficient extent to enable them to displace classroom teaching.

Radio seems to have greatest educational value when used as a supplement to classroom teaching. By means of the radio the best talent—the most outstanding speakers and artists—and material not otherwise available can be brought to the classroom, the school can be kept in close touch with events of the day, interest in public affairs can be created and broadened, appreciation of and interest in the subjects taught in school can be developed, and routine can be broken in interesting and profitable ways. As supplementary to classroom teaching, radio broadcasts have possibilities for enriching education, and are now to some degree serving this purpose.

Radio has much value as a medium for bringing music to people in sparsely settled places or to anyone unable to pay high admission for hearing it. Many people would know nothing of the music of Beethoven, Mozart or Wagner if radio did not bring it to them from the concert halls and the opera houses in which this music is played. Isolation or poverty is no barrier to listening to a composition by any of the masters. Radio not only brings the best music within the hearing of everyone; it today, because of mechanical improvements, also transmits music very satisfactorily.

From the standpoint of amusement, listening to the radio is inadequate diversion because it usually constitutes a passive state; it consists in being entertained, rather than in doing something for one's own entertainment. But the amusement value of active participation on the part of the radio audience is becoming appreciated. Most broadcasting stations occasionally bring people to their studios for the purpose of staging information contests, such as spelling bees or competitive responses to true-false statements, in which the radio audience can in a very significant sense participate. Many radio stations also stimulate listeners to do such things as cast a vote for their favorite entertainer or to comment by letter on the program.

Radio, by means of the auditory impressions it gives, suggests companionship, and so frees isolated persons from much of the feeling of being alone. It does so more than does a book, because the spoken word is evidence of a living human being back of what is said, while the written word is no such evidence. The feeling of being alone is decreased also by hearing the applause of the audience in the sending station, by the conversational method of broadcasting, by being directed to do things, and by knowing that there are thousands of others listening to the same program. And the familiarity of the voices of some of the radio characters and of the announcer makes the listener feel not only that he is in the company of other persons, but that he is in the company of acquaintances. In a questionnaire on the subject, eighty-three per cent of the persons who responded said that, when by themselves, listening to the radio made them feel less lonely.[1]

Although radio broadcasts give a sense of being in the company of other persons, they fall far short of satisfying completely the desire for the presence of other human beings. Persons who feel lonely fly quickly, except when held back in one way or another, from the radio to join a crowd. Group functions in which the social element plays a considerable part are not affected much by the radio. Those who seek the human touch will always regard listening to a broadcast as being less desirable than being actually present at an event that is attended by many persons.

Listening to broadcasts has another disadvantage as compared with actually attending things in that only auditory impressions can at present be sent widely over the air, and so the listener does not see the form and color of the setting from which the broadcast comes. But a skillful announcer gives much vision to the ears, and so makes listening to a program on the air somewhat like taking in the program directly. He may, moreover, get the radio audience to picture in imagination a more interesting setting than actually exists at the sending station.

Listening to radio programs has a number of advantages over going out to take in things in person and may be preferred because of these advantages. In addition to the possible advantage mentioned above, taking in programs by means of the radio saves the inconvenience, the time and the expense of going out. It also makes

[1] Cantril, Hadley, and Allport, Gordon H. *The Psychology of Radio*, p. 102. New York, Harper and Brothers, 1935.

unnecessary the unpleasantness of being bored, for you can always walk out on a radio program without discourtesy to anyone. A broadcast enables you to go unobserved, by anyone outside of the home, to any church, political meeting, theater, or to a prize fight if you care to listen to one. It, moreover, provides many people, as previously stated, with better talent than is directly available to them.

Listening to a broadcast has advantages and disadvantages also in comparison with using a library. Persons on the air seem more real than those in books, but those in books are more frank. Those on the air may also be more personal because their style is more conversational than the usual style of writing. Radio programs consist largely of what appeals to people in general; libraries satisfy every taste. Broadcasts must be taken largely as they come, but reading material may be selected. Listening to broadcasts is easier and less troublesome than is selecting books and reading them, and so those who have no special interests prefer the arranged menu of the air. A book may be read at one's convenience, rapidly or slowly, and when one is in the mood for reading it, but listening to a broadcast is inflexible. In reading a book one can pause to reread; in listening to the radio one must go along with the speaker. Reading requires the entire attention, while broadcasts may be taken in as a background to the doing of other things. Many persons listen while they work. Some housewives, barbers and shopkeepers have the radio turned on most of the day. Even an amazingly high number of college students keep radio broadcasts, especially musical programs, on the air as a background to study.[2] But the use of radio as a background to study does not in itself commend this practice. The way in which a background of broadcasts affects learning can be determined only on the basis of adequate and thoroughgoing investigations of the subject. It may, however, be said that for those whose tasks are long and of a routine character, radio, by making it possible to take in programs while at work, serves a purpose that radio alone can serve.

Radio furnishes the greatest attainable auditory variety. But radio's offerings are varied more to catch the interest of different groups than to please any particular group. To each individual the variety of a series of radio broadcasts is mere variety; variety that is foisted upon him with marked disregard for his taste. The chief evil of broadcasts is that everyone must take the bitter with the sweet, or turn off the radio.

The cries of some advertisers are, of course, the chief annoyance of most radio broadcasts. Advertisers realize this, and many of them try to avoid irritating the listener with direct advertising. They provide "good-will" programs; programs devoted to things of wide interest and in which but brief mention is made of the sponsor's product. Other advertisers, however, feel that the use of the radio is more profitable as a means of direct advertising, and devote much of their time to crying their wares. Should radio advertising become more of the good-will and less of the direct advertising type, listeners would be spared much annoyance.

Radio broadcasts give rise to many severe clashes of interest on the part of members of a household. Children

[2] *Ibid.*, p. 105.

are enthusiastic over programs for which adults have equally strong dislikes. Adults often find their interests in a particular radio program conflicting, and the interest of one adult in listening to a broadcast conflicting sharply with another's interest in reading, conversing or in doing something else about the house. Considerable family irritation originates in clashes of interest in regard to radio broadcasts.

Much of the dislike for broadcasts is due not entirely to their nature, but also to having had an excess of broadcasts. People who must hear radio programs long after they have grown weary of auditory stimulation dislike what might otherwise please them. Radio beats so incessantly upon the ears of many persons that they feel relieved when it is turned off. To keep radio refreshing it is not enough to improve the broadcasts; it is also necessary to prevent over-exposure to them.

Although radio causes much annoyance, it is accepted because of the degree to which it extends and enriches experience.

CHAPTER XXV

CONCLUSION

IN DEALING with people, be ever mindful of man's interest in variety—variety in what you say, variety in your manner of phrasing ideas, variety in the tone of your voice and in the play of your features, variety in what you do in personal matters. In arranging programs for schools, open forums, congregations or social groups, or in designing articles of trade, do not overlook the human interest in having something different for a change. In arranging work and working conditions for employees and in planning recreational programs strive to further the mental health of people and at the same time to prevent much unwholesome behavior by serving the need of variety. In all human relationships and in all human management we should endeavor to make life interesting by providing variety.

> "In this the laws of Nature we obey,
> And follow as her example points the way,
> Which has on every different species thrown
> A shape distinct, a figure of its own;
> Man differs from the beast that haunts the woods,
> The bird from every native of the floods." [1]

[1] Vida, Marco Girolamo. *Art of Poetry,* Bk. III, l. 40. See Albert S. Cook, *The Art of Poetry,* p. 120. New York, G. E. Stechert and Company, 1892.

The greatest variety may be attained through uniformity amidst diversity, as when a drummer in an orchestra beats out repeatedly the same tone while the rest of the members of the orchestra perform an otherwise highly varied composition. It may be attained also through uniformity between series of variations, which arrangement is common in music. What I have said here and elsewhere in this volume about uniformity as a component of the greatest variety may be said in regard to all types of sensory impressions or activity—any experience that consists only of diversity or change, that does not involve some uniformity, lacks the greatest variety. Such an experience may even become boresome. Ruskin said, "The enormous influence of novelty—the way in which it quickens observation, sharpens sensation, exalts the sentiments—is not half enough taken note of by us, and this is to me a very sorrowful matter. And yet, if we try to obtain perpetual change, change itself will become monotonous."

It is not only through uniformity but also, as I stated in some of these chapters and implied in others, through simplicity that variety may be enhanced. After having for some time undergone highly varied sensory impressions, or after having engaged in many different activities, staying at home alone and doing nothing in particular provides novelty. To overlook this fact is to overlook one of the simplest and most effective means of obtaining variety.

In endeavoring to provide variety for others or to obtain variety for oneself a person must not proceed with a blindness to all other values or with indifference toward them; one must not ring in the new that is otherwise bad, nor always ring out the old that is otherwise good. To carry the banner of variety into every phase of life with no thought of other things indicates a simple mind. But in trying to avoid excess beware of satiating others or yourself with sameness, for all that pleases is free of monotony. By providing well-varied experiences for other persons and by achieving well-varied experiences ourselves, we make life for others and for ourselves interesting.

Extensive and detailed consideration was given in this volume to man's want for variety; in the preceding volume, to man's want for a feeling of personal worth. But successful human relationships and human management involve also proceeding with regard for, and providing for due gratification of, man's other wants, in particular the sex want and the want for a livelihood. Accordingly, the same consideration will be given to these two wants in subsequent volumes.

SELF-TESTING EXERCISES

In the writing of this book I applied principles that I discussed in Part One. Some of these applications are referred to below in the first two columns, and principles that they involve are briefly indicated in the third column. Most of the references cited involve more than one principle, but for each reference there is only one principle indicated in the column to the right. Reread each of the references cited below and decide what principle or principles it involves. Then note whether what you have in mind is or includes the principle referred to in the third column. If, as you reread the lines, you do not think of the principle briefly indicated in the third column, even though you may think of other principles that the lines involve, you must consider yourself to have lost in this game with me.

Pages	Lines	Principles Involved
xiv	1-2	images: visual, auditory, temperature, pressure
3	8-9	transposition
3	13	short sentence
4	6-7	figure of speech
4	26-28	imperative sentence
6	21-28	images: visual, heat, smell, cold, pressure, auditory, taste, kinesthetic
8	11ff	developing topic with story
9	19-26	kinesthetic images
11	21-23	parallel construction
13	9	contrast
13	20	short sentence
16	10-11	imperative sentence

Pages	Lines	Principles Involved
17	16-17	paradox
19	19	interrogative sentence
35	21-22	exclamatory sentence
43	19-20	contrast
60	13	auditory images
66	22-23	short sentence
71	13	alliteration
75	25-28	figure of speech
75	28-32	periodic sentence
97	27-30	parallel construction
98	24-31	auditory images
110	32	sentence beginning with adverb
121	19-22	images: kinesthetic, coolness, visual
131	15-18	images: visual, touch, smell, taste
132	6-11	auditory images
133	19-22	contrast
133	19ff	similar sentences
137	28-29	change of emotional state
147	4	interrogative sentence
154	20-25	developing topic with quotation
154	25	irony
167	22ff	overstatement made in light vein
171	18-19	paradox
174	20-23	transposition
204	1-12	sameness: repetition of "variety"; sentences imperative, beginning similarly

In these exercises the correct answers vary from one to all of the items given. Check them.

1. Man desires variety
    a. because of interest in diversity or change.
    b. because of aversion to extreme sameness.
    c. because it is relaxing.
2. The variety that a person has depends upon
    a. the complexity of his experiences.
    b. the number of his experiences.
    c. the agreeableness of his experiences.

d. the degree to which his experiences afford contrast.
e. the degree to which his experiences afford novelty.
3. The desire for variety may be a desire for
    a. change of sensory impressions.
    b. change of independent thought.
    c. change of activity.
    d. change of emotional state.
4. Novelty, to a greater or less degree, is or may be provided
    a. by an unusual experience.
    b. by an unexpected experience.
    c. by any change of experience.
    d. by sameness.
5. Suspense may give variety
    a. by providing change of emotional state.
    b. by stimulating the imagination.
6. In stories, novels or plays, an unexpected ending should leave the individual with a feeling
    a. that he might have expected the ending.
    b. that he couldn't have expected the ending.
7. Leisure was discussed in respect to
    a. the need of relief from boredom with work.
    b. the need of opportunity for doing things of interest.
    c. the amount of leisure needed.
    d. the apportionment of leisure throughout the year.
    e. specific types of leisure activity needed.
    f. freedom in leisure hours.
8. The two purposes of leisure can be served well
    a. by daily intermissions.
    b. by short work days.
    c. by week-ends and holidays.
    d. by annual vacations.
9. A hobby
    a. is needed by everyone.
    b. should always be as different from work as possible.
    c. serves primarily the want for variety.
    d. differs from other forms of active recreation in frequency of pursuit, rather than in kind.

10. Meeting people is often very engrossing
    a. because it involves variety of impression and of expression.
    b. because man is conventional.
    c. because man is intensely interested in his kind.
11. Factors in addition to sameness may influence an individual's attitude toward routine work
    a. favorably.
    b. unfavorably.
12. For reading and independent thought, most people have insufficient
    a. leisure.
    b. privacy.
    c. intelligence.
13. Music and the visual arts may be engrossing
    a. because they afford interesting impressions.
    b. because they afford means of expression.
    c. because they afford more variety than is otherwise attainable by anyone.
14. Contrast in music
    a. may consist of simultaneous tones.
    b. may consist of successive tones.
    c. is less pronounced than in other arts.
15. Poetry provides variety that prose cannot give
    a. because it is different from prose in form.
    b. because it involves unusualness of thought.
    c. because it involves unusualness of manner of expression.
16. Causes of tedium underlying unwholesome behavior are:
    a. monotonous work.
    b. vexatious work.
    c. idleness.
    d. having too much to do.
    e. solitude.
    f. enforced association.
    g. lifelong continuance in monotonous work or living conditions.
17. Types of wrongdoing that may be due to tedium are:

  a. becoming a truant or a vagrant.
  b. starting fires.
  c. engaging in combat.
  d. becoming negativistic.
  e. using alcoholic liquors excessively.
  f. imposing upon another's time.
  g. prying into the affairs of others.
  h. betting.
  i. overstating facts.
18. In bringing about mental abnormality, tedium
  a. is a primary cause.
  b. is a contributory cause.
  c. is a universally recognized cause.

Supply the words needed to complete the following sentences:

1. To give novelty to expression a term used need not be new; it need only to be used in a _____ context.
2. Suspense is a continuous state of ungratified _____.
3. When we enjoy surprise we do so because it gives _____ change of thought or feeling.
4. A monotonous _____ is less boresome than a monotonous _____ because it leaves the mind freer.
5. Most people have an insufficiency of _____ recreation, rather than of _____ recreation.
6. The emotions stressed in this book as means of providing variety are _____, _____, and _____.
7. Travel may be enjoyed because it provides change of _____ and novelty of _____.
8. In all of the arts it is not simply variety, but unified _____ that is pleasing.

INDEX

Age, and interest in variety, 106–107
Art, as a means of enlarging experience, 185–189

Bennett, James V., 116
Boileau-Despréaux, Nicolas, 179, 180, 181
Bryant, William C., 121
Burns, Robert, 29

Cantril, Hadley, 199
Carlyle, Thomas, 159
Catt, Carrie Chapman, 24
Change of scene, experienced during leisure hours, 167–168; experienced in pursuing occupations, 169–170; need of providing opportunities for, 170
Contrast, in discourse in general, 25–26; in dramatic works and stories, 26–27; in nature, 132; in poetry, 179–180; in art, 186; in music, 192
Copeland, Helen, 45
Cowper, William, 112, 131, 180
Curiosity, change of emotional state provided by, 35; activity aroused by, 35–36; general statements illustrating appeals to, 36–38; periodic sentences illustrating appeals to, 38

Deceptiveness of novelty, 107–108
Development of subject in different ways, 28–29
Dickens, Charles, 46

Edison, Thomas Alva, 152
Emerson, Ralph Waldo, 19

Familiarity, preferred to novelty, xiv, 18, 110, 205
Figures of speech, variety provided by, 31–32; other purposes served by, 31

Gillilan, Strickland, 59

Hamilton, G. V., 101
Hobbies, definition of, 147; by whom needed, 147–148; different from work, 150; similar to work, 150–151; type needed, 151
Hobhouse, S., 86
Hogarth, William, 187, 188
Holmes, Oliver Wendell, 9
Humor, unexpectedness in, 57–59

Individuality, maintainance of, 14, 69
Ingersoll, Robert, 29–30
Irving, Washington, 109

Johnson, Samuel, 48, 94, 113

Kline, Linus W., 93

Leisure, why needed, 125; daily intermissions, 128; short working days, 128–129; week-ends and holidays, 129; annual vacations, 129–130; freedom during, 153ff.
Lin Yutang, 133–134, 136–137
Lindeman, Eduard C., 146, 156

Lorentz, Pare, 38
Lowell, Amy, 88
Lowell, James Russell, 14

Masefield, John, 181–182
Meeting people, variety attained in, 158; interest in, 158–162; providing opportunities for, 163–166
Mental abnormality due to tedium, 100–102
Mental pictures, providing variety of, 29–33, 179; in figures of speech, 31; in single words, 32; aroused indirectly, 32–33
Movement, in discourse, 8–9
Music, as a means of enlarging experience, 190–195
Myerson, Abraham, 96–97

Nature, variety afforded by, 131–138; bringing the individual in touch with, 138

Occupations, for engaging the mind and body, 112–116; gainful, 112–113; therapeutic, 113–116; change of, 116
O'Reilly, John Boyle, 44
Originality, in discourse, 3, 178; in dress, 68; in the doing of things in general, 68–75
Overstatements, made in a light vein, 4–5; made seriously to attract attention, 100

Parallel construction, variety provided by, 24
Poetry, as a means of enlarging experience, 178–184
Pope, Alexander, 181, 195
Precision, variety afforded by, 17, 24–25, 64–65
Privacy, need of, 154, 176–177

Radio, as a means of enlarging experience, 196–202; compared with other means of communication, 197–201
Reading and independent thought, as means of attaining variety, 171–176; providing privacy for, 176–177
Renner, George T., 23
Robinson, Edwin Arlington, 180–181
Ruskin, John, 204

Sameness, affording variety: in sentence structure, 23–24; in work, 120–123; in experiences in general, 109, 204
Saxe, John G., 98
Shakespeare, William, 56, 109, 190
Silence, variety provided by, 11, 34
Simplicity, variety provided by, 109, 204
Sorenson, Herbert, 88
Sprague, Charles, 35
Steiner, Jesse Frederick, 144
Surprise, in paradoxes, 49; in irony, 51; in stories and plays, 52–55; in comparisons, 56–57; in humor, 57–59
Suspense, variety experienced during, 40–43; interest sustained by, 43–44; disappointment resulting from incorrect anticipation during, 45; exploitation through arousal of, 46

Tedium, causes of, 79–90

Unity, in discourse, 9–10; in nature, 135; in art, 187; in music, 191
Unwholesome behavior, 91–102

Vida, Marco Girolamo, 4, 178, 184, 203

INDEX

Weaver, Andrew Thomas, 66
Wenner, Margaret, 70
Whitman, Walt, 131, 161, 179, 194
Window with a view, need of, 138
Wordsworth, William, 154
Works Progress Administration, 145–146, 156
Wyatt, S., 81, 117